Making the Most of Being Mentored

Mentors help. Mentees do.

Second Edition

Gordon F. Shea
Stephen C. Gianotti

A Crisp Fifty-Minute™ Series Book

AXZO ✿ PRESS

Making the Most of Being Mentored

Mentors help. Mentees do.

Second Edition

Gordon F. Shea
Stephen C. Gianotti

CREDITS:

President, Axzo Press:	**Jon Winder**
Vice President, Product Development:	**Charles G. Blum**
Vice President, Operations:	**Josh Pincus**
Director, Publishing Systems Development:	**Dan Quackenbush**
Copy Editor:	**Catherine M. Albano**

Trademarks

Crisp Fifty-Minute Series is a trademark of Axzo Press.

Some of the product names and company names used in this book have been used for identification purposes only and may be trademarks or registered trademarks of their respective manufacturers and sellers.

Disclaimer

We reserve the right to revise this publication and make changes from time to time in its content without notice.

ISBN 10: 1-4260-1837-1
ISBN 13: 978-1-4260-1837-4

Printed in the United States of America

2 3 4 5 6 7 8 9 10 13 12 11 10

Table of Contents

About the Authors

Gordon F. Shea is the author of 15 books and over two hundred articles on subjects such as: organizational development, leadership/management, communications, team building, and workforce development. He has published dozens of articles on mentoring in periodicals such as the *Managing Diversity Newsletter, Supervision, Women in Computing, Bottom Line Business,* and the *Commandant's Bulletin* (U.S. Coast Guard).

Stephen Gianotti is the founder and CEO of The Woodland Group, LLC, specializing in individual, group, and organizational diagnostics and development. For 30 years he has authored hundreds of development programs for multiple industries across the United States as well as internationally. He is a frequent a keynote speaker and workshop facilitator at national conferences and was recently reinvited to be one of three judges for the "Best Firm to Work For," a national recognition for companies that create and sustain supportive and productive work environments. Stephen specializes in executive coaching, mentoring, strategic on-boarding, and workplace interpersonal dynamics, and he has authored year-long leadership development programs for emerging and experienced leaders.

Preface

This book is designed to complement the Crisp Series book *Mentoring: A Practical Guide*. While *Mentoring* focuses on mastering the knowledge, skills, and practices of successful mentors, this book offers exercises, information, and self-study activities for those who are or intend to become involved in a mentoring relationship as a mentee.

Like any relationship, the mentoring relationship is most effective and most healthy when mentees understand that they are involved with a process in which they can, and should, influence its daily course and its overall outcomes. *Making the Most of Being Mentored* puts forth a foundation for building this awareness and the skills that will enable mentees to achieve the maximum benefit from the commitment s/he makes to this valuable opportunity.

This book also deals with many practical aspects of the mentoring relationship, such as assessing what the mentee is able and willing to invest in the relationship, the challenges of various mentoring situations, as well as how to transition the relationship once the official mentoring is over.

The way mentoring used to be thought of, there was an assumption that what the mentor says is the most important part mentoring. Of course, this is only half of the equation. The other half is using the richness of what the mentee says as well.

I wish you the best of luck in your learning journey. May you realize success in each and every mentoring experience that you participate in. Each one can change a life—quite possibly yours—and can play a role in changing an organization.

American President Barack Obama said during his inaugural address on January 20, 2009:

> *Hope is... the belief that our destiny will not be written for us, but by us; by all those men and women who are not content to settle for the world as it is; who have courage to remake the world as it should be.*

Mentoring carries with it that same hope that the relationship provides the courage to remake individual worlds as it can be—to realize its full and true potential.

Stephen C. Gianotti

Objectives

Complete this book, and you'll know how to:

1) Explore how a mentoring relationship can be beneficial to the mentee, the mentor, the organization and, possibly, to friends and family members.

2) Discuss the responsibilities of mentees in managing their own personal development and career growth.

3) Explain the skills needed to foster successful mentoring partnerships.

4) Provide guidance on building and maintaining productive mentoring relationships.

5) Identify techniques for maximizing results and using new skills to contribute to the success of the organization.

Workplace and Management Competencies mapping

For over 30 years, business and industry has utilized competency models to select employees. The trend to use competency-based approaches in education and training, assessment, and development of workers has experienced a more recent emergence within the Employment and Training Administration (ETA), a division of the United States Department of Labor.

The ETA's General Competency Model Framework spans a wide array of competencies from the more basic competencies, such as reading and writing, to more advanced occupation-specific competencies. The Crisp Series finds its home in what the ETA refers to as the Workplace Competencies and the Management Competencies.

Making the Most of Being Mentored covers information vital to mastering the following competencies:

Workplace Competencies:

▶ Teamwork

Management Competencies:

▶ Supporting Others

▶ Motivating & Inspiring

▶ Developing & Mentoring

For a comprehensive mapping of Crisp Series titles to the Workplace and Management competencies, visit www.CrispSeries.com.

About the Crisp 50-Minute Series

The Crisp 50-Minute Series was designed to cover critical business and professional development topics in the shortest possible time. Our easy-to-read, easy-to-understand format can be used for self-study or for classroom training. With a wealth of hands-on exercises, the 50-Minute books keep you engaged and help you retain critical skills.

What You Need to Know

We designed the Crisp 50-Minute Series to be as self-explanatory as possible. But there are a few things you should know before you begin the book.

Exercises

Exercises look like this:

EXERCISE TITLE

Questions and other information would be here.

Keep a pencil handy. Any time you see an exercise, you should try to complete it. If the exercise has specific answers, an answer key will be provided in the appendix. (Some exercises ask you to think about your own opinions or situation; these types of exercises will not have answer keys.)

Forms

A heading like this means that the rest of the page is a form:

FORMHEAD

Forms are meant to be reusable. You might want to make a photocopy of a form before you fill it out, so that you can use it again later.

A Note to Instructors

We've tried to make the Crisp 50-Minute Series books as useful as possible as classroom training manuals. Here are some of the features we provide for instructors:

▶ PowerPoint presentations

▶ Answer keys

▶ Assessments

▶ Customization

PowerPoint Presentations

You can download a PowerPoint presentation for this book from our Web site at www.CrispSeries.com.

Answer keys

If an exercise has specific answers, an answer key will be provided in the appendix. (Some exercises ask you to think about your own opinions or situation; these types of exercises will not have answer keys.)

Assessments

For each 50-Minute Series book, we have developed a 35- to 50-item assessment. The assessment for this book is available at www.CrispSeries.com. *Assessments should not be used in any employee-selection process.*

Customization

Crisp books can be quickly and easily customized to meet your needs—from adding your logo to developing proprietary content. Crisp books are available in print and electronic form. For more information on customization, see www.CrispSeries.com.

The Heart of the Mentoring Relationship

> **The illiterates of the 21st century will not be those who cannot read and write, but those who cannot learn, unlearn, and relearn."**
>
> —Alvin Toffler

In this part:

▶ The Trio Definitions

▶ The Benefits of Being Mentored

▶ Mentoring in the Past

▶ Mentoring Today

▶ The Trend Continues

▶ Mentor–Mentee Mutuality

▶ The Essence of Mentoring

▶ Realizing Potential

▶ The Mentoring Commitment

The Trio Definitions

At the very beginning of our journey we should define terms for this book. Three terms we will use frequently are *mentoring*, *mentor* and *mentee*. Below are the working definitions that we will use.

Mentoring is a personal or professional relationship. Its main objective is a developmental experience in which a more experienced person guides the development of a less experienced person. Mentoring includes a high level of interpersonal communication and is relationship-based. The mentoring relationship can include some or all of the following:

▶ Formal or informal conveying of knowledge

▶ Social connections or networking

▶ Psychological or social support

Mentoring is a developmental caring, sharing, and enabling relationship in which two people collaborate by investing their time to enhance growth, knowledge, and skills. The best mentoring responds to critical needs in a person's life in ways that prepare for greater performance, productivity, or achievement in the future.

A *mentor* is a trusted advisor—someone who usually is a more experienced person in business or in life. In the business context, employees are paired with more experienced people, who coach, council, and advise them and serve as a form of role model. Mentors help individuals advance their careers, add to their education, and help build or add to their networks.

A mentor can have a long-lasting effect on another person, generally as a result of personal one-on-one contact. A mentor is one who offers:

▶ Deeper knowledge

▶ Keener insight

▶ Broader perspective

▶ More wisdom

▶ Wider connections

A *mentee* is the recipient and beneficiary of a mentoring relationship. In traditional workplace environments this was the younger of the two people. Today, age is no longer a critical factor.

The mentee—sometimes referred to as protégé—makes an effort to:

- ▶ Assess knowledge
- ▶ Internalize knowledge
- ▶ Effectively use the knowledge
- ▶ Increase skills
- ▶ Gain insights
- ▶ Add perspective
- ▶ Develop (more) wisdom

Mentoring has changed over time; its importance and impact have not. That is why it is still a key strategic tool for forward-thinking, competitive organizations.

When people talk about the mentors they've had, they almost always describe people who affected their lives in important, long-lasting, and especially productive ways. These mentors often helped their mentee turn an important corner, opened new vistas for them, or helped them see themselves in a new and improved way. The relationship may have been brief or extended, yet it was long enough to help the benefiting individual change and improve from that day forward. The mentor might have been a parent, a teacher, a neighbor, a friend, or anyone else who helped make a powerful, lasting change in someone's life.

The mentee is usually the predominant beneficiary of the relationship. But when done well, a healthy, well executed mentoring relationship benefits both parties, often for a lifetime.

This book focuses primarily on the role of the mentee.

"Should I refer to you as 'Mentor Mine'?"

WHY COMMIT?

Why might you as a mentee want to commit to a mentoring relationship? What is the list of development areas that you would like to partner with someone to work on? What specific areas or topics do you find exciting, valuable, rewarding, or broadening if you are mentored by the right person?

_____

_____

_____

_____

What are the characteristics that you would like to have in a mentor to realize the items that you listed above? What kinds of things would you want the mentor to bring to the mentoring relationship? Be specific.

_____

_____

_____

_____

What characteristics do you bring to the mentoring relationship? Be specific.

_____

_____

_____

_____

Be clear about what you want and about what you bring to the table.

The Benefits of Being Mentored

As you review this list of benefits, think about the previous exercise and see how these match what you hope for in the mentoring experience. Check which ones are important to you. Next, circle the ones that are "must haves" in the mentoring relationship.

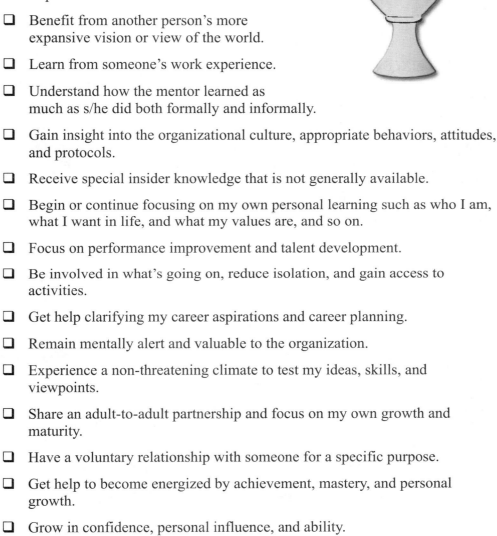

- ❑ Benefit from another person's more expansive vision or view of the world.

- ❑ Learn from someone's work experience.

- ❑ Understand how the mentor learned as much as s/he did both formally and informally.

- ❑ Gain insight into the organizational culture, appropriate behaviors, attitudes, and protocols.

- ❑ Receive special insider knowledge that is not generally available.

- ❑ Begin or continue focusing on my own personal learning such as who I am, what I want in life, and what my values are, and so on.

- ❑ Focus on performance improvement and talent development.

- ❑ Be involved in what's going on, reduce isolation, and gain access to activities.

- ❑ Get help clarifying my career aspirations and career planning.

- ❑ Remain mentally alert and valuable to the organization.

- ❑ Experience a non-threatening climate to test my ideas, skills, and viewpoints.

- ❑ Share an adult-to-adult partnership and focus on my own growth and maturity.

- ❑ Have a voluntary relationship with someone for a specific purpose.

- ❑ Get help to become energized by achievement, mastery, and personal growth.

- ❑ Grow in confidence, personal influence, and ability.

Review this list to move toward being as clear as possible about what you want from a mentoring relationship. Sometimes we think of mentoring as having only one goal or one outcome. Perhaps this list will help you expand your goals and outcomes so that you can maximize your time with your mentor.

Read the case study below and then answer the questions in the following exercise.

CASE STUDY: Randy Learns about Learning

My name is Randy Eddington. I was hired as a wi-fi technician to do customized in-home and commercial installations for an Internet service provider. Three months later Kevin was assigned to be my mentor. He said his job was to help me keep my skills up-to-date. He asked where I wanted to be in five years. I was caught without a clear response as I didn't know what to say. At that time I thought a job was a job as long as I got paid, and there wasn't much more to it. Kevin said that my skills would be outdated in six to eighteen months and I'd eventually be unemployed if I didn't invest in my own continuous professional development. That scared me, so I said that I wanted to learn but didn't know how to even begin to think about planning a career path.

He had me fill out several forms and exercises to provide feedback about myself and my abilities and strengths. After we reviewed the results, he introduced me to several people who had also done extensive wi-fi installations and had gone on to more complex and better-paying work. Now I'm enrolled in my second computer language certification course and have come to believe that education is no longer a finite concept. Learning for me will always be part of my life. I even noticed it helped my personal life as well.

What do you think Randy learned that was significant?

_____

_____

_____

What are some things that helped Randy learn them?

_____

_____

_____

Who would you say are the mentors in the Randy story?

_____

_____

CONTINUED

━━ CONTINUED ━━

In what ways does Randy now think differently?

_____

_____

What do you think Randy's professional life will be like in five years?

_____

_____

INFLUENCE EXERCISE

Relate one situation where you started to change your attitude, behavior, or values based on discussions you have had with another person:

_____

_____

_____

How do you think the situation might have turned out if you hadn't had this person's help?

_____

_____

_____

_____

66

Three keys to more abundant living: caring about others, daring for others, sharing with others."

–William Arthur Ward

Mentoring in the Past

In the United States, cultural norms and workplace norms have evolved over the years. Prior to our current Global, Green, Information-Age, High-Tech Era, many economies and cultures were based upon what was known as the Industrial Revolution or Industrial Era. The machine-age Industrial-Era organization was characterized by:

1. A many-layered, hierarchical structure that concentrated power and authority almost exclusively at the top of the organization.

2. Slow and difficult decision-making procedures, often with many sign-off steps and layers of bureaucracy.

3. Decisions made at the top without adequate knowledge of, or concern for, organization-wide consequences resulting in "fixes that fail" or "unintended consequences."

4. Operational and strategic thinking and decision making considered to be nearly the exclusive responsibility of staff experts or managers.

5. Highly structured organization where there was a clear chain of command. Going outside the chain of command was not good for one's career.

6. The common assumption that moving up in the organization was the only way to go and the only way that had value.

7. The belief that only high performers needed or deserved to be mentored.

8. The belief that insider information and who you know are the essential factors in getting ahead.

9. The assumption that anyone in management had the qualifications to be a mentor.

10. More focus on individual career development and less understanding of organizational development as a whole entity or system.

11. Working hard and keeping your nose clean as a means to job security.

The way mentoring was done in the industrial era might have benefited those institutions, but times have changed. Before we discuss those changes complete the following brief exercise.

INDUSTRIAL ERA REFLECTION

Let's assume that you worked for an industrial era organization that had the characteristics shown in the list on the previous page. Using the list and your imagination, what might working for that organization be like?

_____

_____

_____

_____

If you received mentoring at that organization, what might the experience of mentoring be like? Again, use your imagination and think about the kind of environment that you would be mentored in and how that environment might impact your mentoring experience.

_____

_____

_____

_____

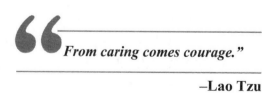

From caring comes courage."

—**Lao Tzu**

Mentoring Today

Those who began their careers in an industrial era workplace have had to adjust to how work is accomplished in today's global, green, information-driven, high-tech era. They might need to replace outdated beliefs, behaviors, and attitudes with those that are more relevant in today's workplace.

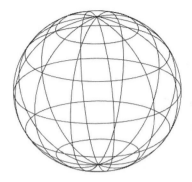

Many of those currently entering the workforce know only the current standards and are not bound by the old ways of doing things. These two extremes present an opportunity for different mindsets to learn from each other. Mentoring can help workers adapt and learn the best practices.

The global, green, information-driven, high-tech era is characterized by:

1. Fewer layers of management: a "flat" organizational structure.

2. A more flexible, adaptive, and change-oriented culture.

3. Mentoring used as a key strategic tool for workforce development, career and succession planning, and personal growth.

4. The use of mentoring as a competitive recruitment and retention tool.

5. More decision making by those closest to the customer and closest to where the actual work is done.

6. Seeking and supporting ideas throughout all organizational sectors.

7. Fast tracking the flow of skills, knowledge, and ideas from the point of origin to where they are needed.

8. Active search for diversity of thought, demographics, and skills.

9. A more deliberate process for matching mentees with mentors who have the expertise and abilities for a successful mentoring experience.

10. Increased willingness and ability to communicate throughout the organization at all levels and at multiple locations, often globally.

11. The concept of job security is based more on mutuality and the value that a person is able to (continually) add.

Mentoring in today's workplace is vastly different from how it was done in the industrial era. Before we discuss those changes, complete the following brief exercise.

GLOBAL, GREEN, INFORMATION-DRIVEN, HIGH-TECH-ERA REFLECTION

Let's assume that you work for a global, green, information-driven, high-tech-era kind of organization that has the characteristics listed on the previous page. Using the list and your imagination, describe what would working for that organization would be like.

_____

_____

_____

_____

If you received mentoring at this global, green, information-driven, high-tech-era organization, what would the experience be like? Again, use your imagination if you need to and think about the kind of environment that you would be mentored in and how that environment might affect your experience.

_____

_____

_____

_____

What are the differences?

As you compare this exercise and the one before it, what are the differences between the two mentoring experiences? Which in your opinion would have the greater impact? Why?

_____

_____

_____

_____

The Trend Continues

For years corporate recruiters have been asked by job applicants for many types of industries if prospective employers have a mentoring program. For some potential employees and many employers, it is a critical part of their corporate culture.

Most employees today want four basic things from work. They want:

▶ To feel like they are part of something larger than themselves

▶ To do work that has meaning to them and to the organization

▶ To be appropriately recognized for the value they add

▶ To have a sense of the future and their place in it

Effective mentoring keeps these in mind as the relationship evolves. Effective mentoring can positively impact each of these dramatically. Many mentoring conversations revolve around one or more of these basic elements.

In today's downsized, flat, and lean organizations, many employees have felt a strong shift or change in their organizations. Colleagues who might once have been in the next cubicle are now in another country. The team that used to think, look, and act alike now features diversity of appearance, thought, and action. This continued shifting of organizational makeup could actually increase the need for personal contact with others whom they can trust and from whom they can learn and feel some degree of connectivity. Being mentored can address these very real needs in today's workplace.

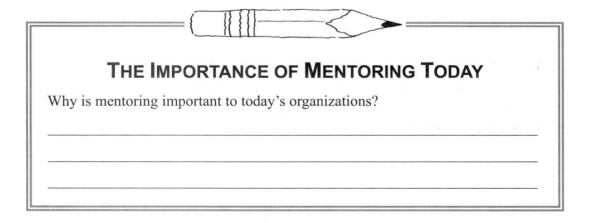

THE IMPORTANCE OF MENTORING TODAY

Why is mentoring important to today's organizations?

_____

_____

_____

Never believe that a few caring people can't change the world. For, indeed, that's all who ever have."

–Margaret Mead

Mentor–Mentee Mutuality

Today's mentoring relationships are expected to be a lot more like an adult/adult relationship than the industrial era's parent/child model.

Parent/child relationships tend to be hierarchical, with the parent in total control and the child being directed. Micromanaging is quite typical in a parent/child relationship. Permission to act is required; non-initiative is the general rule of thumb.

An adult/adult working relationship is just the opposite. Each person is responsible for taking initiative. There is little need for "permission" and more discussions about options, possibilities, taking risks, and entertaining "what if" scenarios. adult/adult kind of relationship is based on a common sense of "mutuality."

The term "mutuality" refers to a relationship that is reciprocal in nature and provides a two-way flow of:

▶ Responsibility   ▶ Accountability

▶ Benefit   ▶ Respect

▶ Enjoyment   ▶ Caring

In a mentoring relationship, mutuality means agreeing on a set of behaviors that will govern how both parties will mentor together, instead of having the mentor simply call the shots.

Before we leave the concept of mutuality, let's clarify some of the things that mentoring is not. Mentoring is NOT:

▶ A training program—but training might be part of mentoring.

▶ A temporary worker program—but the mentee might be assigned to work in a different locale as part of mentoring.

▶ A social club—but there are social elements in an effective mentoring relationship that quite often expands the mentee's network.

▶ Psychotherapy—but there is listening to problems both professional and personal. Leave the psychological analysis to the professionals.

▶ Necessarily a friendship—but quite often friendships are formed and many last a lifetime.

▶ Merely a transactional contract—it is meant to be a means to truly connect with another human being.

The best form of mentoring occurs when the participants transcend daily transactional work and delve into the deeper aspects of who they are and who they aspire to be.

CASE STUDY: All in the Family

Chanda was the youngest of six children of a family that emigrated to the United States. Upon graduation from high school, Chanda expected to follow the family tradition in which girls married and raised children. All of Chanda's siblings considered high school to be the end of education, except for Gaurang. He joined the Army after high school, achieved a bachelor's degree while in the service, and learned a skill that was transferable to civilian life.

After Chanda graduated from high school, Gaurang engaged her in a private conversation. He said he was disappointed in her for accepting the traditional family expectations for her future. He said she was too bright and talented for such a limited role in life, one based on cultural and sexual stereotypes of what women could and couldn't do. Chanda said the conversation lasted less than 30 minutes.

The next day Chanda enlisted in the Air Force without telling her parents or discussing her plan with anyone. Now in her mid-thirties, she is happily married, has four children, is employed as a top-level director at an investment firm, and holds an MBA. Chanda considers her brother's intervention just what she needed at the time—powerful mentoring.

Today Chanda says, "My brother Gaurang challenged the way I was thinking about my life and my future. His words had an enormous impact and forced me to think carefully about the assumptions I was making. My life has changed for the better because I didn't just follow family tradition."

The Essence of Mentoring

Truly effective mentoring is usually a cascade of "gifts" from the mentor. Mentors typically make very personal and special efforts, encouraging mentees to use imagination to move beyond what they have seen or experienced. At their best, mentors go beyond initial expectations and provide the mentee with valuable gifts that last a lifetime.

Below are some factors that can influence whether someone might transition to the role of a mentor.

▶ Mentoring focuses on the needs of the mentee and an effort to enable the mentee to meet those needs.

▶ Mentoring often operates on a "just-in-time" principle where the mentor offers the right help at the right time. A mentor must recognize an opportunity when it presents itself.

▶ Much of what the mentor offers is personal learning or insight, which is rarely written down. The mentor may not be aware of what he or she can offer until a mentee expresses a need and the mentor realizes there might be a match with something they know.

▶ Mentoring requires giving beyond giving. Many people think twice about adding such a commitment to their busy lives. However, if they choose to do so, the rewards of personal achievement, mentee appreciation, and a sense of helping to build a better organization can be enormous.

Effective mentors offer their own strengths and abilities. These might include:

▶ Job, career, or personal coaching that stretches the mentee's thinking

▶ Work and life experiences

▶ Access to a network of personal and professional contacts

▶ Knowledge of emerging trends or developments within the organization or industry

▶ Guidance with developing and implementing personal development plans

▶ Serving as a role model

Certainly this list is not exhaustive. What are some other elements that a mentor might provide a mentee?

MENTORS IN MY LIFE

More than likely each of us has been mentored in our lifetime. It is also quite possible that we didn't know it at the time that we were being mentored. This exercise asks you to look back and identify some people who have gone beyond performing their job or carrying out responsibilities in order to help you. List the person's name and provide a one-sentence description of how that person affected you.

A teacher: _____

Impacted me by: _____

_____

A coach: _____

Impacted me by: _____

_____

A counselor: _____

Impacted me by: _____

_____

A friend: _____

Impacted me by: _____

_____

A relative: _____

Impacted me by: _____

_____

> *There is no better way to thank God for your sight than by giving a helping hand to someone in the dark.*
>
> **–Helen Keller**

Realizing Potential

Mentoring promotes the belief that there is potential in every human being. A person's untapped potential might include attributes that the person is not even aware of. The best mentoring relationships can unleash this untapped potential so that mentees can:

▶ See it, perhaps for the first time.

▶ Understand its power.

▶ Use it to better themselves and others.

There are many reasons why a person might not be aware of their own potential. For example, children of dysfunctional families often grow up without a positive self-image. People from challenged economic backgrounds might not have access to opportunities to better themselves. This world is full of people whose talents and abilities exist only as potential until they are mentored. Mentoring therefore can empower the mentee.

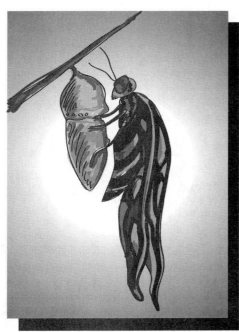

Empowerment helps others overcome their difficulties, challenges, disadvantages, blind spots, or deficiencies, so that they have a chance to discover their talents and create better lives. How do mentors do this? Mentors engage in a dialogue and caring relationship that centers on the mentee's potential. Doing this can bring to the surface one or more mentee needs. Once the mentee's needs are "on the table," a good mentoring relationship collaborates to meet those needs and to realize that potential.

This can lead to constructive, live-altering effects. A successful mentoring relationship is not easy, but it is less difficult than it seems to empower people to change their own lives.

The Mentoring Commitment

Take a moment and think back over your life. Think about what you consider to be major events. One such even could be graduation. Another could be marriage or your first or new job. List them below.

Some Major Events in My Life

Chances are, each of these events was preceded by some kind of effort, involvement, and/or commitment. In the case of a new job, there is usually considerable effort to obtain that job. Significant things rarely come about without purposeful effort. While most of us realize this, human beings usually need frequent reminders of this simple formula.

Idea + Mental Commitment + Time Commitment = Realized Potential

In a mentoring relationship, there is nothing more powerful than the commitment that both the mentor and mentee make to each other and the relationship. This commitment needs to be very clear, up-front, and consistent.

Never underestimate the power of two people who are aligned in their commitment to something. Great things can happen when this occurs.

Making the Most of the Commitment

After you commit to a mentoring relationship, the journey to new and life-changing places can begin. Each person has a critical role to play in making sure that the commitment supports and feeds the mentoring relationship. By playing these roles with sincerity, each person supports the relationship and builds a solid foundation for success.

Mentees support the relationship by:

▶ Being willing and able to share their ideas and needs with their mentor

▶ Articulating their ideas, thoughts, difficulties, and needs clearly

▶ Becoming at ease with their mentor

▶ Being willing to trust and to open up

▶ Being willing to being influenced

▶ Making a choice to develop and change themselves

Mentors can support the relationship by:

▶ Offering time selflessly

▶ Sharing a network of knowledgeable and experienced contacts

▶ Providing constructive feedback

▶ Being the best listener possible

▶ Not taking over by trying to do what the mentee should be doing

▶ Being more a guide and less a director

What do you think are some additional things that both mentor and mentee can do to support the mentoring relationship?

What the Mentee Can Do	What the Mentor Can Do

CASE STUDY: Ellie's Network

Ellie worked for a year as a buyer at a small retailer. Last summer she moved to another city to take a job in the purchasing department of a government agency. Because of her limited experience, she was offered an entry-level position.

Her new supervisor, Jose, said that he would be pleased to mentor her if Ellie would define her work-related objectives and identify specific areas in which she needed help, such as government procedures or laws under which the agency operated.

As Ellie's supervisor began to teach her the essentials of the job, the two would meet for the last 30 minutes of each work day. When they started doing this, Jose insisted that Ellie share any problems she encountered on the job. Together they worked out ways to resolve these issues. At least 10 to 15 minutes of each meeting was centered on what Ellie wanted to achieve in this and future jobs. The sessions were quite gratifying for Ellie and raised her awareness of how complex it was to work for the government in this type of environment.

Just as Ellie was getting her feet on the ground, Sandy, a co-worker, invited her to join the local chapter of the Purchasing Agents Association.

That same day she found an e-mail message from Dell, a purchasing agent in another region, offering to go through the purchasing process with her, step by step, and cover the exceptions as well. Dell said he would "help mentor Ellie for success."

When Ellie mentioned these coinciding events to her supervisor, Jose replied, "It is no coincidence; we laid plans the day you reported for work. Your professional associations will also provide you with a 'network of mentors' as you successfully master one area after another."

Answer the following questions based on this case study:

1. What is the impact of having a network of mentors (multiple people providing you mentoring-like experiences)?

_____

_____

_____

CONTINUED

2. What, if any, potential disadvantages might there be of having multiple mentors?

_____

_____

_____

3. What techniques might Ellie use to overcome any of the above disadvantages? (Hint: stress management techniques, establishing her own agendas for the sessions, etc.)

_____

_____

_____

4. Ellie agreed with Dell that their mentor/mentee relationship would be carried on via e-mail, texting, Skype, Twitter, and FaceBook, as needed. How can they use these tools most effectively?

_____

_____

_____

5. What precautions should they exercise in using these tools?

_____

_____

_____

> *Three helping one another will do as much as six men singularly."*
>
> **–Spanish Proverb**

Part Summary

In this part you learned the definitions of **mentoring**, **mentor**, and **mentee**. Next, you learned the **benefits** of being mentored. You learned how mentoring functioned in the **past**, and how it is different **today**. Then, you learned the value of mentor-mentee **mutuality**. You learned how mentoring can help a mentee to realize **potential**. Finally, you learned about the **mentoring commitment**.

The Proactive

Mentee

We make a living by what we get; we make a life by what we give."

–Winston Churchill

In this part:

- ▶ The Mentee as Collaborator
- ▶ Inviting a Mentor to Collaborate
- ▶ Managing Your Own Development
- ▶ Our Own Motivation & Sense of Self-Determination
- ▶ The Value of Being an Active Learner
- ▶ Making a Habit of Lifelong Learning
- ▶ Creating a Flexible Life Plan
- ▶ Shifting Your Mental Context
- ▶ Staying Flexible

The Mentee as Collaborator

In the previous chapter we discussed the workplace of the Industrial Age. It would be safe to say that many of those employees were more passive than active. It was typical for employees of the Industrial Age to be skilled at only one task and educated to the point of being able to get the work done and not much more. In a time that saw much labor unrest, management preferred a passive and obedient workforce. Back then, mentoring—if it occurred at all—was for technical, professional, or management personnel.

By contrast, in today's Global, Green, Information-Driven, High-Tech Era, mentees might have mentors who possess fewer academic degrees than they do. A mentor might have less cross-cultural experience than the mentee. Such mentees can still benefit from the mentor's particular and specialized knowledge, quality experience, organizational insight, and industry connections. It is also not uncommon for a younger person who has special know-how to mentor an older person who happens to need what the younger colleague possesses. This is referred to as "reverse mentoring."

Whatever the specifics of the relationship, that relationship succeeds through collaboration.

Collaborate, Collaboration, & Collaborator

The "Triple C's"—These three words in many ways typify a mentoring relationship. What a mentoring relationship does (the verb) is collaborate. What the mentoring relationship is (the thing) is a collaboration. Each person—mentor and mentee—is a collaborator.

Collaborate—the Action of Mentoring

"To work jointly with others or together especially in an intellectual endeavor"

The word itself is composed of three parts:

►   *co*: meaning "together"

►   *labor*: meaning "work"

►   *ate*: inferring a collective body

Taken together, the loose translation could be "laboring together as one unit."

A mentoring relationship takes place between two people who retain a certain amount of independence while being committed to each other. Some companies still use the older ways of mentoring, but many organizations employ a high level of mutuality for the basis of developing more mature, adult-to-adult, productive mentoring relationships.

Collaboration—The Essence of Mentoring

Collaboration is a good word to summarize what a mentoring relationship is. It is a partnership between two people.

Collaborator—The People of Mentoring

A collaborator (within a mentoring relationship) defines both people. The mentor and the mentee that have made a commitment to each other.

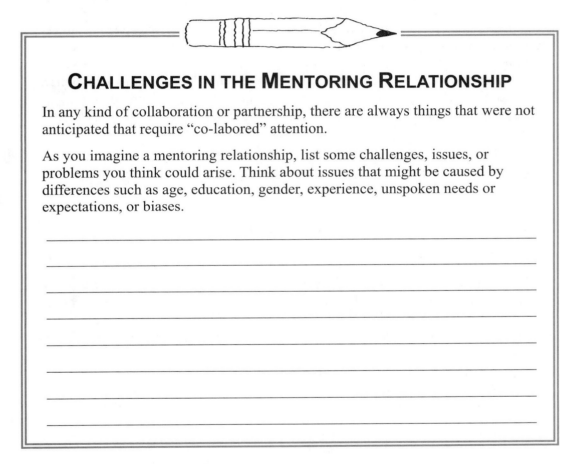

CHALLENGES IN THE MENTORING RELATIONSHIP

In any kind of collaboration or partnership, there are always things that were not anticipated that require "co-labored" attention.

As you imagine a mentoring relationship, list some challenges, issues, or problems you think could arise. Think about issues that might be caused by differences such as age, education, gender, experience, unspoken needs or expectations, or biases.

_____

_____

_____

_____

_____

_____

_____

_____

_____

And in the end, it's not the years in your life that count. It's the life in your years."

–Abraham Lincoln

Inviting a Mentor to Collaborate

When we approach another person to be our mentor, we are asking that person to give of themselves, usually for free. Formal mentoring programs commonly provide the mentors—usually by asking for volunteers. The fact that enormous numbers of people do sign up to mentor for free, reflects the goodwill that leads to healthy, helping relationships of various kinds.

As altruistic as most Mentors are, most have expectations about the relationship. It is possible that these expectations are not conscious and only become so after an expectation is not met. Some of the things that a mentor might be expecting from the relationship could be:

1. A sense that they are making a constructive difference to their mentee's life.

2. Some expression of appreciation or acknowledgment of the mentor's effort.

3. An enjoyable relationship.

As a mentee, there are several things you can do to encourage a mentor's interest in working with you. While you might not have all of these answers, sometimes inviting a mentor to be a partner in finding these answers serves as a good invitation.

▶ Articulate what you need or want from the relationship.

▶ Define your objectives.

▶ Identify potential issues that might get in the way.

▶ Anticipate what a mentor could do to help you.

▶ Don't ask for special favors above and beyond the limits of the relationship.

▶ Have a plan for reaching your objectives.

▶ Build a high level of relationability between you and your mentor.

▶ Be able to state why what you want matters.

These topics become easier if the mentoring is arranged by your employer. Once these items are clear, finding the right mentor becomes much easier.

Managing Your Own Development

In many organizations, the pace of operations, intensity of competition, and continual change in technology have led to a culture of "employee-driven" (not employer-driven) career development. This means that more employees are being asked to take charge of their own development.

This doesn't mean that organizations have chosen not to support employee development. The trend has been for a while now that today's organizations define their corporate goals and objectives and expect employees to develop themselves in ways that support those goals. This implies that to continue adding value each employee needs to assume greater accountability for his/her own self-development. Nimble and competitive businesses depend on employees to upgrade their skills and prepare for their future in alignment with the needs of the organization.

The more successful organizations make it clear that managers need to support the employee's efforts by making resources available and to coach and advise as needed. A proactive employee who has an unsupportive manager might be handicapped in the mentoring process.

PROACTIVE CAREER-BUILDING

Write a brief paragraph describing how you might become more proactive in building your own career.

_____

_____

_____

_____

_____

_____

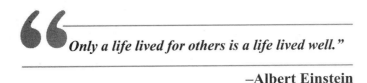

Only a life lived for others is a life lived well."

—**Albert Einstein**

MENTORING BENEFITS CHECKLIST

A successful mentee takes action to get the most out of a mentoring relationship. Review this list and check the items that would be beneficial to your development.

- ❑ Learn techniques for strengthening personal health and wellness
- ❑ Develop win-win negotiating skills
- ❑ Keep an ethical and moral compass within the business world
- ❑ Strengthen communication skills (writing, speaking, listening)
- ❑ Invest time and effort in helping others (demonstrated caring)
- ❑ Practice team-building skills
- ❑ Practice bringing people to consensus
- ❑ Pursue deeper levels of job knowledge and skills
- ❑ Acquire and practice trust-building skills and behaviors
- ❑ Exercise to enhance physical strength, energy, and stamina
- ❑ Identify personal negative habits and reduce them
- ❑ Develop and practice assertiveness (versus aggressive) skills
- ❑ Practice sharing your ideas, skills, and knowledge more broadly
- ❑ Learn and practice conflict resolution/management skills
- ❑ Strengthen one's character by study and application
- ❑ Improve problem identification, analysis, and decision making
- ❑ Master techniques for better managing of personal stress
- ❑ Improve time management
- ❑ Practice positive self-projection (in speech, dress, self-image, and so on)
- ❑ Seek ways to broaden personal vision and imagination
- ❑ Search for ways to enhance interpersonal sensitivity and awareness
- ❑ Relish and use positive and constructive humor
- ❑ Develop positive affirmations about one's constructive attributes
- ❑ Practice enhanced levels of optimism and positive thinking
- ❑ Take initiative more often

PRIORITIZING MENTORING BENEFITS

Now that you have reviewed items that might be beneficial to your personal and/or professional development, let's take the next step. Below you are asked to do three things.

1. List the five benefits that you believe will be the most beneficial to you right now.

2. Write a brief sentence stating why it is important to you.

3. List what you think you might need to accomplish this item.

Top Five Item	Why It's Important	What You Might Need
1.		
2.		
3.		
4.		
5.		

Our Own Motivation & Sense of Self-Determination

Imagine a company where the performance evaluations were somewhat unique. Each time your evaluation showed that you did something really well, your manager received a high rating and not you. To make this even more interesting (and perhaps more crazy), imagine that if your evaluation showed an area in need of improvement, you alone were held responsible for the unacceptable performance. This fictitious story is meant to drive home an obvious point: employees need and deserve recognition for their work. This recognition can be a motivating force.

Imagine the effect on an employee's morale and performance if recognition is not a part of the performance evaluation or part of the corporate culture. Attitudes within the organization might sound something like: "Why bother if someone else is going to get the credit for my hard work?"

Many firms now realize the value of allowing employees to make decisions regarding their work *and* recognizing them for it. Doing this can lead to:

► A greater confidence level

► A more self-driven willingness to take responsibility

► A sense of satisfaction often displayed as enthusiasm.

The combination of allowing people to take on a greater role in decision making and then rewarding them helps create and maintain "self-determination" or control. In all relationships, we need to feel we have some level of control. Our sense of control is directly related to motivation. If we don't feel like we have control, we tend to say, "Oh, what's the use!"

The issue of our own (internal) motivation is fundamental in our personal and professional lives. Work dynamics often employ a "carrot and stick" mentality. The carrot is a metaphor for being motivated by something we want. The stick is a metaphor for being motivated by something we don't want or are afraid of. Even today in our Global, Green, Information-Driven, High-Tech Era, there remain some management mentalities that fear should drive employee performance more than reward. The truth of the matter is, you get what you reward and recognize.

Employees usually make a clear, often conscious, choice to accept or reject the carrot or the stick. We have resoundingly found that the carrot works much better both short and long term and companies that have been repeatedly recognized as the "Best Place to Work" have this as part of their core values and corporate culture.

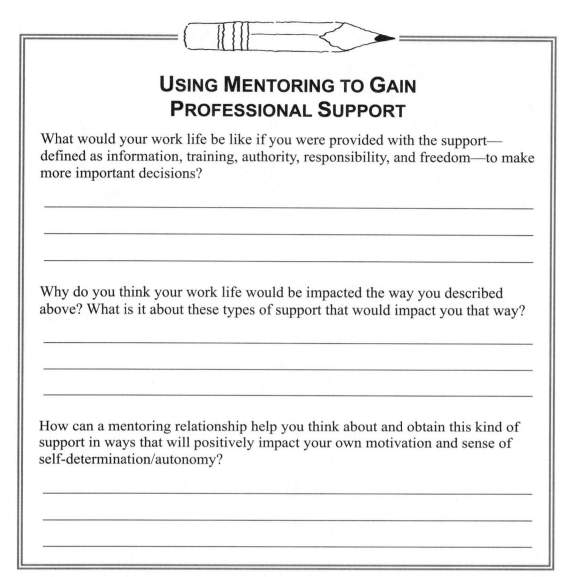

USING MENTORING TO GAIN PROFESSIONAL SUPPORT

What would your work life be like if you were provided with the support—defined as information, training, authority, responsibility, and freedom—to make more important decisions?

_____

_____

_____

Why do you think your work life would be impacted the way you described above? What is it about these types of support that would impact you that way?

_____

_____

_____

How can a mentoring relationship help you think about and obtain this kind of support in ways that will positively impact your own motivation and sense of self-determination/autonomy?

_____

_____

_____

_The most decisive actions of our life…
are most often unconsidered actions._"

–Andre Gide

The Value of Being an Active Learner

At the beginning of a mentoring relationship, some mentees might think they will be spoon-fed new information and learning. Some mentees expect to be "sponges" for information that will be dispensed by a mentor, who knows just what to say and do. The kind of sponge-only learning is called *passive learning.* When compared to the opposite, *active learning,* passive learning is the less effective way to go for either the mentor or the mentee.

Active (or assertive) learners are highly motivated and act upon that motivation in ways that lead the mentoring process. Leading the process might look like:

- ▶ Fully articulating what they want to accomplish

- ▶ Sharing their needs and goals with their mentor

- ▶ Keeping the relationship on track by…

    - ▷ Asking for feedback

    - ▷ Providing feedback

    - ▷ Asking for clarity when something isn't clear

    - ▷ Requesting time

    - ▷ Managing the time

- ▶ Testing understanding by restating what was heard

- ▶ Rewarding and recognizing the mentor

- ▶ Making note of progress and things learned

- ▶ Showing an eagerness for continued, possibly faster, progress

Of course, the mentor has to help moderate the active learner so that the mentee doesn't (on purpose or unconsciously) try to take over the relationship and void its mutuality. A mentor needs to fuel a mentee's fire but not let it rage out of control.

An active learner does not sit around waiting for rewards to fall out of the sky. Nor is an active learner so demanding that the mentor is stretched too thin or begins to feel resentful because requests are stacked too high. Active learning is assertive, but it is *appropriately* assertive. The mentor and the mentee discuss an appropriate level of assertiveness. This underscores the foundational and critical nature of this collaborative relationship built on mutuality.

GAINING KNOWLEDGE IN YOUR FIELD

How would you define your learning style? Are you more of a passive or active learner?

_____

_____

_____

Describe recent efforts you have made to keep current in your field, to better understand your work or profession, or to follow trends and developments that might affect your future professional well-being.

_____

_____

_____

List the names of people from whom you have gained important knowledge for your personal OR professional well-being and development. Who were they and what did you learn from them?

_____

_____

_____

What are some ways that you can increase your being an active learner as much as possible?

_____

_____

_____

> "_Life's challenges are not supposed to paralyze you; they're supposed to help you discover who you are._"
>
> **–Bernice Johnson Reagon**

Making a Habit of Lifelong Learning

Many of us view the current Global, Green, Information-Driven, High-Tech Era as full of excitement, opportunity, and challenge. Many other people find it full of change, uncertainty, and insecurities. No matter where you are on this spectrum, lifelong learning will be necessary if you want to thrive in the workplace.

As a mentee, there is a great deal you can and need to do to continually feed yourself educationally, experientially, and intellectually. Take the initiative to make the most of your mentoring opportunity. Raise insightful questions, conduct research and homework, and take the extra steps to take full advantage of the range of gifts your mentor brings.

In addition to helping your career, there is a physical reason why lifelong learning makes sense. Numerous studies find that the brain is essentially a muscle and the more you exercise it, the more chances you have to live healthier, longer, and more rewarding life.

TURNING INTEREST INTO A CAREER

Identify the hobbies, extracurricular activities, interests, or pastimes that you have enjoyed and possibly others that you might enjoy as subsequent careers.

_____

_____

_____

Of these, which ones do you have the greatest interest or talent in?

_____

_____

What would it be like for you to turn one of these interests into an actual career at some point in your life?

_____

_____

_____

Creating a Flexible Life Plan

Before the current Global, Green, Information-Driven, High-Tech Era, organizations were designed to maintain status quo. There was a perception that keeping things relatively the same was a competitive advantage. People were discouraged from changing careers or even employers. A person was expected to pick a career early and pursue it to retirement. Career consultants described this as *linear life plan*.

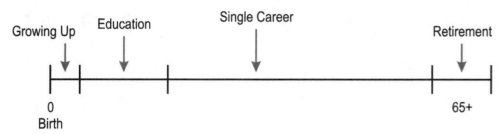

Linear Life Plan Model

Today, the linear life plan no longer fits reality. The concept of retirement and retirement age have dramatically changed. In some cases, retirement age has been pushed back due to long life spans; for others, it might be the shifting economic times and the real financial need to work more years. Many people enjoy the work they are doing and therefore work beyond the traditional retirement age. Some people have multiple careers in a lifetime. A flexible life plan (versus the linear life plan) is the reality of today's global workplace.

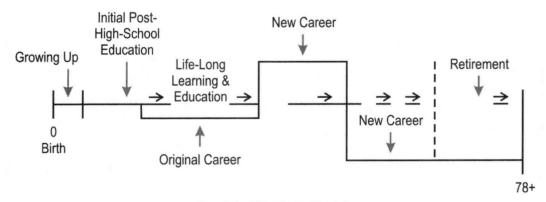

Flexible Life Plan Model

Shifting Your Mental Context

A woman faced a job counselor and said, "I'm a laid-off social worker." This woman understandably identified herself only by her work and by her employment situation. She could have said, "I am a career transition social worker who is considering exploring new ways of investing my talents." Clearly both comments provide insight as to how she sees herself. Both are also true statements. The latter presents greater potential.

How we define ourselves and our jobs directly impacts our psyche and our level of hope. Don't ignore or deny a situation that requires focused energy. We do believe that our "self-talk"—the verbal proof of our mental context—can make the difference between getting out of a hole or staying in it.

Mental context shifting means thinking differently about our goals or the tasks of a job. It is an effective way to help us learn. Why? Because shifting how we think opens us up for different possibilities and greater opportunities.

▶ It can produce personal motivation to learn new material.

▶ It can strengthen retention so that the positive effects of learning increase over time.

▶ It helps us to take responsibility for reinforcing our own learning.

The pace of change in most organizations is so great that entire positions can be eliminated or dramatically changed by a single technological advance or an unexpected swing in the global economy. These kinds of changes can be initially difficult on many, but can create opportunities for those who can do mental context shifting. Personal versatility and adaptability are "must haves" in today's world.

ENLISTING A MENTOR

As a mentee, how can you enlist the help of one or more mentors to help you make your mental shift even more effective?

_____

_____

_____

_____

_____

Staying Flexible

Managers have long claimed that "people resist change."
While this might sound true, the reality is that human beings
are quite adaptable to change. Many would argue that human
beings were designed for change. We certainly do change over
the course of our lives, don't we?

Actually, people are not inherently resistant to change. People
are resistant to being confused by change. When change makes
sense to us, we embrace it. For example, if we buy a new
house that we really want, we don't resist this kind of change. When we go to
college or get a new job, these are changes that we don't resist. When we see gain,
no serious loss, and/or fully understand the change, we accept it much easier.

Regardless, change can often involve stress. This can range from "good stress" such
as winning a game or getting a new job, to distress, such as being laid off or losing
your car keys. If stress in any aspect of life becomes too intense, lasts too long, or is
repeated too often, it can cause physical damage. Thus, significant, sustained, or
adverse change may well generate resistance.

In an era when your skill, a certain technology, a specific job, or an entire
organization can become suddenly obsolete, the need to adapt successfully and
quickly goes way beyond important. It is an essential life skill. Increasingly,
organizations are on the lookout for versatile, adaptable, and creative individuals.

We know for a fact that our bodies need to be exercised in order to operate at
maximum capability. The same is true for our inner self in terms of bending and
stretching and being nimble when it comes to change.

"I'm his mentor."

YOUR ADAPTABILITY SCALE

Circle a number on the top and the bottom scale to indicate how you historically have responded to job-related change in the past.

Rigid, Unyielding	1	2	3	4	5	6	7	8	9	10	Flexible, Adaptable
Find Change Threatening or Disturbing	1	2	3	4	5	6	7	8	9	10	Very Accepting of Change

Where might inflexibility keep you from adapting to the organization's needs?

_____

_____

In the areas that you identify as inflexible, why do you think you are that way and what are the outcomes of your being that way?

_____

_____

_____

What might be some things you can do to overcome this specific resistance?

_____

_____

_____

How can the mentoring relationship help you in these areas?

_____

_____

Life is like an onion: You peel it off one layer at a time, and sometimes you weep."

–Carl Sandburg

CASE STUDY: Turning Adversity into Opportunity

At 32, James is a design engineer at a global Internet search firm. He began his career there shortly after graduating from college at 24. Last Friday James was caught in the company's latest wave of downsizing and now had two weeks before he was unemployed.

The company offered those who were laid off small severance package of four weeks pay and one week of pay for every year employed. James really enjoys design work and while the severance will be helpful, financially he still has to work. A week after he was laid off, James sat down to outline a personal "rest-of-my-life" plan.

One idea James had was finding a mentor. He had been assigned to a technical mentor when he first joined the company. The mentor's perspective, experience, and wisdom had a profound and beneficial effect on James's professional behavior, his sense of the engineering art, and his passion for his work. James believed that additional mentoring could help guide his future. He planned to take the following steps:

▶ Contact several design engineers who had been doing work similar to his and who had found good work with good pay since leaving the company.

▶ Contact several younger engineers to find out what's "hot" in the job market and what he'd need to do to get current.

▶ Establish a network of mentors via LinkedIn and Plaxo who could provide personal insights into the current job market.

▶ Ask for referrals and connections to other professionals who could provide specific assistance and mentoring while he defined his emerging needs.

▶ Identify career alternatives such as entering other fields of work, consulting opportunities, temporary work, and moonlighting—particularly options that would expand his skills and knowledge.

▶ Scour the Internet for jobs beyond his usual geographic boundaries and entertain more global opportunities and connections.

CONTINUED

■ CONTINUED ■

If something similar happened to you and you decided to seek help from mentors, you should develop a plan to deal with your new situation. Below are some items that might help you with such a plan.

1. What specific types of mentoring would be helpful to you under these conditions?

   _____

   _____

   _____

   _____

   _____

2. What types of mentors would you seek? (For example, former co-workers who have been re-employed, people who could give you insight on how you might want to redirect your life or career, individuals familiar with changing attributes of the workplace, and so on.)

   _____

   _____

   _____

   _____

   _____

3. How would you approach these potential mentors to gain their assistance and support?

   _____

   _____

   _____

Life is a succession of moments. To live each one is to succeed."

–Corita Kent

Part Summary

In this part, you learned how to view the mentee as a **collaborator** in the mentoring process. Then you learned how to **invite** a mentor to collaborate. You learned how to manage your own **development**, your own **motivation**, and your sense of **self-determination**. Next, you learned how to be an **active learner** and to make learning a **lifelong habit**. You learned how to create a **flexible life plan**. Finally, you learned how to shift your **mental context** and to stay **flexible** and adaptable.

Seven Critical

Mentee Skills

> *Believe that life is worth living, and your belief will help create the fact.*"
>
> –Henry James

In this part:

▶ Identifying Effective Mentee Skills

▶ Skill 1: Ask Productive Questions

▶ Skill 2: Develop Triple-Level Listening Skills

▶ Skill 3: Use Trust as Your Glue

▶ Skill 4: Overcome the Awe Factor

▶ Skill 5: Resolve or Manage Differences

▶ Skill 6: Capture the Gifts of Learning

▶ Skill 7: Internalize the Learning

Identifying Effective Mentee Skills

Mentoring is based on the concept of mutuality, so it is important to emphasize skills that the mentee brings to the relationship. This does not refer to technical skills, but the skills the mentee needs to successfully establish and maintain a mentoring relationship.

Old ways of mentoring might focused less on what the mentee brings to the table and more on having the mentor do most of the work. This is no longer the case in today's workplace. The exercise below will help identify specific mentoring-related skills that a mentee needs to bring to the relationship.

YOUR MENTEE SKILLS

Identify any skills you think might be helpful to you in serving as a mentee:

_____

_____

_____

_____

_____

As you review the skills you wrote above, which ones do you think you do best and least? We would strongly suggest that you discuss these above with your mentor, your supervisor, or even other mentees.

_____

_____

_____

_____

_____

EVALUATING COMMUNICATION HABITS

Mentees can become more involved in their own development through a bit of self-reflection. The quiz below identifies key interpersonal communication areas of a mentoring relationship. Please take a few minutes to complete this brief quiz.

Rating scale: Always = 10, Frequently = 8, Usually = 6, Seldom = 4, Never = 2

When meeting with your mentor do you:

_____ 1. Communicate clearly?

_____ 2. Welcome your mentor's input (express appreciation or say how it will benefit you)?

_____ 3. Reveal your important feelings about the subjects discussed?

_____ 4. Accept feedback?

_____ 5. Practice openness?

_____ 6. Take initiative to maintain the relationship with your mentor?

_____ 7. Actively join in to explore options with your mentor?

_____ 8. Share results of things you learn with your mentor?

_____ 9. Hear the whole message including mentor's feelings?

_____ 10. Remain alert for a mentor's non-verbal communications and use it as data?

_____ **TOTAL**

If you scored 70 or below, you likely would benefit greatly by practicing the mentee skills that follow. If you scored 80 or better, you already possess good mentee interaction skills.

Have your mentor complete this quiz about you and then compare your scores. This could be helpful in clarifying impressions and assumptions.

Skill 1: Ask Productive Questions

Rudyard Kipling wrote in his *Just So Stories*, "I have six honest serving men / they taught me all I know / Their names are What? and Why? and When? and How? and Where? and Who?"

If you can get those questions answered (and keep asking them as appropriate) you can learn a great deal. Asking good questions provides one of the best avenues to probe more deeply into the learning opportunities at hand.

Because mentoring is a relationship based on mutuality, it presents an opportunity to gather facts for problem solving. What better way to engage in problem solving than to first ask questions? These questions can be a potent tool and can help your mentor get to the heart of what you need to know.

The quality and quantity of your questions can make a difference. Open-ended questions, those that cannot be answered by a simple "yes" or "no," usually trigger a more substantial discussion compared to closed questions that are answered by a one-word response. Deep conversations result from open-ended questions. So, productive questions are those that stimulate substantive and relevant information flow and exchange.

Example:

> **Closed**: "How many months will the program operate?"
>
> **Open**: "What level of commitment is expected for those participating in this program?"

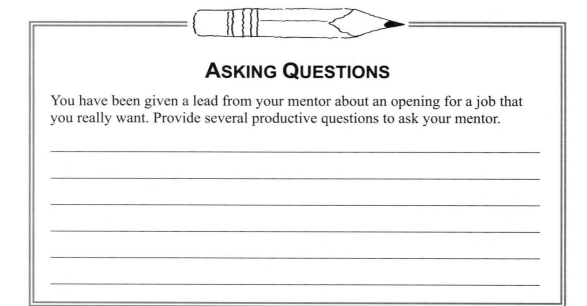

ASKING QUESTIONS

You have been given a lead from your mentor about an opening for a job that you really want. Provide several productive questions to ask your mentor.

_____

_____

_____

_____

_____

_____

Skill 2:
Develop Triple-Level Listening Skills

Active listening is a key component to any healthy relationship. When we actively listen, we are listening at multiple levels. The first level is listening to the *words* that are being said. The second level is listening for the *emotion* attached to the words. The third level is listening for the *intent* or the deeper message.

In a perfect world we would operate at 100% for each of these levels. Being mere mortals, we don't always listen that well. Sometimes we miss the feeling. Sometimes we miss key words. Sometimes we hear the feelings and the words but we miss the overall meaning of what the person is trying to say.

Triple listening involves a high level of concentration and discipline. This means work. Effective listening requires focus and energy to be able to fully hear and truly understand what is being said.

There is a saying that goes, *"People want to know that they have been heard more than they want to be told they are right."* As you practice triple listening, be careful not to judge or take sides or tell people they are right or wrong. The most important thing you can do when listening is to understand what people are really trying to say.

Five tools for improved triple listening:

▶ Summarize what you heard.

▶ Determine the personal value in what the mentor is saying.

▶ Identify and eliminate "blank spots."

▶ Use inquiry rather than advocacy.

▶ Be open to influence.

Summarize

As you listen, focus on central themes or ideas. After you have listened to the person, reflect back to the person what you think you heard by saying, "So, what I heard you say was…." By summarizing this information, you convey the critical message that you heard what was said.

Personal Value

Once you have clarified the central idea, consider how it applies to the mentoring relationship and in particular to you as the mentee. This will let the mentor know you are applying what was said to your life situation. It will also tell the mentor how "on target" the message was.

"Blank Spots"

When we listen to someone, we have a reaction. These reactions can range from good to bad to neutral. Sometimes our reactions can cause psychological blank spots. These blank spots can cause us to leap to assumptions or react in ways that are inappropriately emotionally charged. This compromises our ability to hear what is really being said. Be aware of your reactions to what is being said. The best listening first recognizes and then manages emotional responses appropriately.

FINDING YOUR BLANK SPOTS

To become more aware of words that might trigger your blank spots, keep track of your next few conversations—with anyone—to see what words or phrases trigger an emotional response in you. Write a couple of them below and challenge yourself to find out what triggered you.

_____

_____

_____

_____

Inquiry and Advocacy

When listening to another person, you may be tempted to judge or evaluate what is being said. The next time you listen to someone, try to respond with questions instead of advocating a position. Remember that the purpose of listening is not to judge or offer corrections or solutions. That is problem solving. The purpose of listening is simply to understand.

Openness to Influence

Try to remain open to others' influence and ideas. During a conversation we may be inclined to certain kinds of reactions. For example, if we are talking about changing a marketing plan, I might not be open to suggestions if I am heavily invested in the current plan. In this case, I am not open to being influenced. I could be closing off a source of new information or new ideas.

There are many ways that you can improve your listening skills. We have offered several here that we have found very helpful in the mentoring relationship. Can you think of additional tools to improve your own listening?

Skill 3: Use Trust as Your Glue

People think about trust differently, but it would be to say that trust is important to all of us. In terms of trusting others, most people fall into two categories.

Group One
I assume trust until you give me a reason not to trust you.

Group Two
I will trust you after and only until you prove you are worthy of my trust.

Regardless of which group you consider yourself to be in, the goal in a mentoring relationship is to maximize the level of trust. The more trust there is, the safer we feel about sharing thoughts, hopes, dreams, and what we need or want.

Certain behaviors can positively or negatively impact a relationship's level of trust. As you review the pairs of behaviors below, consider which ones you use and how it might impact your life and any mentoring relationships.

Trust-Building	Trust-Lessening
Encourages	Discourages; puts people down
Helps others	Looks out for self; selfish
Listens	Listens but doesn't hear what's said
Shares ideas, thoughts, and feelings	Hides ideas, thoughts, and feelings
Speaks frankly and directly	Indirect, vague, or devious
Verbal and nonverbal congruency	Actions differ from words; sends mixed signals
Cooperates	Competes; stresses winning
Acts as equal	Acts superior
Appropriately acts confident, self-assured	Insecure, fearful; takes lead from others
Gets close physically or psychologically	Remains distant; separate physically or psychologically
Freeing and allowing	Controlling

Trust-Building	Trust-Lessening
Caring	Unconcerned
Friendly	Standoffish, uninvolved
Accepts, tolerates most behaviors	Critical, judgmental
Transparent, open, aboveboard	Covert, underhanded, sneaky
Unconditional; open to new ideas and information	Convinced, close-minded, opinionated
Concentrates on resolving conflicts and interpersonal problems	Threatens, punishes, and acts vindictive
Empowers and builds people up	Cuts others down; insults, ridicules
Treats people as individuals	Categorizes and stereotypes
Accentuates the positive	Stresses deficiencies and negatives
Acts calmly under stress	Explodes, overreacts
Acts spontaneously, authentically	Selfishly strategizes, manipulative
Empathetic	Indifferent, cold, distant

TRUST-BUILDING BEHAVIORS

Review the trust-building behaviors and consider how you might work on them to build trust in your mentoring relationship. List those you will begin to work on and how you will go about doing that. Who can help you?

_____

_____

_____

_____

_____

Skill 4: Overcome the Awe Factor

You might be mentored by someone you hold in very high esteem. In the extreme, if a financial manager was to be mentored by Warren Buffet or if Michele Obama was to mentor someone in raising children, that mentee might feel a bit overwhelmed by the perceived gap between them. When a mentee is in awe, the relationship might be slow to get started. At some point the mentee and mentor need to find a relatively even playing field so that the "fame" or "awe" factor does not get in the way of what the mentoring relationship is intended to accomplish.

Research shows that when the awe factor affects a mentoring relationship, mentees may be reluctant to truly engage in the relationship. These mentees often failed to set developmental objectives for themselves, develop significant agenda items for their meetings, or take initiative during these sessions. Mentees in this situation told researchers that they:

▶ Were afraid to make mistakes in front of their mentors

▶ Had trouble viewing their mentors as partners

▶ Often considered their own problems and needs to be insignificant

This research also showed that mentors tended to rate these same mentees as lacking initiative, as followers rather than as leaders, and as poor performers.

Believing that "there are important people…and then there are the rest of us" can create a self-defeating attitude. Remember, famous people, rich people, well-known politicians, highly skilled doctors, successful bankers—and the list goes on—all have one thing in common with you and me. They are all people. And because they are all people, that can be part of the glue that binds a mentoring relationship.

The "awe" factor is very common and quite understandable. As with anything else that gets in the way of an effective mentoring relationship, this "awe" stuff needs to be put on the table, talked about, and then put aside so the business and benefits of mentoring can begin.

OVERCOMING AWE

What would be your reaction to being mentored by someone famous and/or someone you hold in very high regard?

_____

_____

_____

_____

_____

Why do you think your reactions would be as you describe them above?

_____

_____

_____

_____

If you think you might be a victim of the "awe factor," what do you think you could do to make this a non-issue or at least a smaller issue?

_____

_____

_____

_____

_____

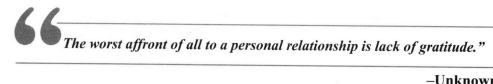

The worst affront of all to a personal relationship is lack of gratitude."

–Unknown

Skill 5: Resolve or Manage Differences

It would be naive to think there won't be differences in a mentoring relationship. In every relationship, the partners will see things differently at some point. For the sake of this learning point, let's call this difference *conflict.*

Avoidance Is Not an Option

First, let's normalize the term *conflict.* If we automatically think that all conflict is bad, we will probably short-change ourselves in the benefits of mentoring. Conflict by itself is neither good nor bad. What makes it good or bad, helpful or hurtful is how the conflict is dealt with, and this must be determined by the mentor and the mentee.

We recommend several techniques to deal with conflict. You can confront your mentor about what he or she is doing or not doing. However, even in situations where it would be helpful to clarify or resolve differences, many mentees are reluctant to take the initiative. Mentees may be concerned that they will not handle the situation well, they might be perceived as adversarial, or the relationship might be damaged.

Do a Mental Context Shift

As mentioned earlier, how we think makes a critical difference in any conversation or relationship dynamic. If you avoid conflict because you fear it or think it can only hurt or damage a relationship, then we would suggest that you do a mental context shift to change that thinking.

The realities are:

▶ Whether you think conflict is good or bad, chances are you are right. So think positive. It's your choice.

▶ Failing to deal with conflict often destroys a relationship.

▶ Dealing with conflict later versus earlier generally causes more damage and is more difficult to deal with.

▶ Sometimes the best you can do is to manage conflict. Not all conflict can be resolved.

▶ Effective conflict resolution or conflict management very often has the effect of deepening relationships, not damaging them.

The Soft Response

When you feel a conflict or difference is in the air, one way to address it is to use the soft response. The soft response is way to bring a topic up in a non-threatening way that doesn't alienate or offend the other person.

Examples:

> *That advice bothers me, but I'm not sure why.*

> *That might be a good idea, but it doesn't fit my way of doing things.*

The goal of soft responses is to invite a discussion of why the suggestion might not be applicable for you or why you might have difficulty carrying it out. This should lead to better understanding between the mentee and mentor.

"I" versus "You" Messages

Another effective tool that usually carries a low risk of damaging the relationship is called an "I" message. The purpose of the "I" message is to focus on yourself rather than to place blame on the other person.

> **You message**: *You didn't show up for our meeting yesterday.*

> **I message**: *I had put on my calendar that we were meeting yesterday.*

The "I" message requires you to think about what happened and to frame the message in a way that is not accusatory or blaming. It also forces you to consider that maybe you might be mistaken about what happened. This is a good exercise, particularly when you are initially convinced that you are in the right.

An "I" message generally consists of three parts:

▶ Non-blaming description

▶ Statement of effects

▶ Statement of feelings

Non-blaming Description

This description should be neutral and objective in nature. Developing a non-blaming description of another person's behavior, when they have done something important enough to you to talk to them about it, is extremely difficult for most people.

Example:

> *In order to attend our weekly meetings, I drive to work rather than take the bus.*

Statement of Effects

This is a statement of the tangible and concrete effects on you, now or in the future.

Example:

> *This means I have to pay to park near the office. Then I have to pay a second time when I return from our meetings.*

Statement of feelings

This is a statement of your feelings or emotions about what happened.

Example:

> *Whenever possible, I'd like to schedule meetings a day in advance so I can take the bus rather than drive on days we are not meeting.*

The main thing to remember here is that when discussing a potentially contentious issue, the more you use the word "you," the higher the likelihood that the other person will feel accused or blamed.

While this specific tool doesn't come with a money-back guarantee, it can help immensely when there is a touchy issue that needs to be put on the table.

Not Giving Advice

In mentoring, one factor that can create conflict between partners is the expectation that the mentor should give advice. However, experience and research have shown that giving advice can have a negative impact. Why would that be?

Let's say that a mentor gives the mentee advice and the mentee acts on it. Ideally, it was good advice and the mentee benefited from a good decision. What would happen if the advice was bad, or wasn't fully informed? What if the mentee misinterpreted the advice or altered it? As you can see, there are way too many variables for advice to be used as tool for consistently positive outcomes. Here are a few examples of giving advice.

> *I think you should...*
>
> *I can solve your problem better than you can, so let me tell you how...*
>
> *If I were you, this is what I would do...*

Instead of advice, the mentor should guide the mentee's own search for a solution or decision. Mentor advice could take away the motivation for the mentee to find the best answer and, most importantly, *own* that answer. Teaching mentees to find their own answers feeds the learning and maturation process.

Working out Problems

A mentoring relationship often becomes a close professional relationship, so it's no surprise that occasional difficulties arise between mentor and mentee. It is helpful for a mentee to remember that the mentor is there to help, guide, and challenge. If problems are going to be resolved successfully, the outcome has to include a win-win approach. This places responsibility on both partners to find ways to create positive outcomes for difficult issues.

HANDLING ADVICE

Describe one experience you have had with advice from any source for whatever reason.

_____

_____

_____

_____

If you followed the advice, what were the outcomes?

_____

_____

_____

If you didn't follow the advice, why not and what did you do instead?

_____

_____

_____

What are some of your reactions to this section (Skill 5: Resolve or Manage Differences)?

_____

_____

_____

Skill 6: Capture the Gifts of Learning

"No sleeping" could be one of the mottos to help guide you through your mentoring relationship. That means stay sharp. Realize that every interaction with your mentor can be a gift of learning. If the saying below is true…

Every passing minute is a chance
to turn it all around.

…then being unaware or "sleeping" during your mentoring experience could prove costly in terms of missed opportunities. Alertness, involvement, and careful active listening are all essential to benefit from a mentor's gifts, whatever form they are in.

There will be times when you will need to sort the necessary from the dispensable, the unusual from the ordinary, or the powerful from the trivial. There are some specific actions that can help you capture the essence of your mentor's gifts and "stay awake."

1. Ask yourself at the end of each mentor/mentee meeting, "What did I learn today?" Be sure to share this with the mentor. Share it with others as well. Chances are every meeting will have a learning moment for you.

2. Ask yourself, "How can I apply what I learned?" Be sure to write a plan as brief or as involved and detailed as you need it to be so that you will actually do it. Share this with your mentor.

3. Ask questions about anything you experience in a given day that seems important to you. Write them down when they happen so you won't forget them.

4. Listen carefully to your mentor's feedback. Be open-minded. Watch out for defensiveness.

5. Show appreciation for your mentor's time. The best way to keep a good thing going is to reinforce it.

Being present, totally present, is not an easy task. In this society, we can be very distracted by important things that don't matter right now. Right now is all that matters when you are with your mentor. Stay focused, alert, engaged, proactive, candid, open, grateful, and most of all, aware that you are being given a gift.

Skill 7: Internalize the Learning

There are a number of ways to take what we have learned and make it stick or internalize it. The simple four-step process below might help with your relationship.

1 In your learning, what patterns emerged? What things kept coming up about where you can grow? Seek your mentor's input on this.

2 Review sooner versus later. The longer you wait to reflect or review your learning, the more you lose. There tends to be a substantial loss of detail one to three hours after a learning experience.

3 Record the outcome of each mentoring session. Use digital recordings, send yourself an email, create your own blog, or draw diagrams—whatever process works best for you. The critical thing is to capture the learning in some tangible way.

4 Discuss ideas, viewpoints, and other attributes of the learning with another person. Another way to reinforce or internalize the learning is to either share it with someone or try to teach it to someone else.

"As your mentor it's disturbing that I'm the only one taking notes."

RETAINING LEARNING

How do you currently manage to review and retain what you learn from others?

_____

_____

_____

When you learn, observe, or experience something that is important to remember in detail, what techniques will you use to internalize or "make stick" that learning so it becomes part of your behavior in some positive way?

_____

_____

_____

PRACTICING POSITIVE BEHAVIORS

The following eight behaviors will help a mentee succeed in the mentoring relationship. Answer each question yes or no. If yes, give a specific example. If no, think about something you can do, a technique to use, a behavior you can modify, or a resource you can consult to turn your "no" into a "yes." Record your plan in the space provided.

1. I set realistic expectations with my mentor. ❑ Yes ❑ No

_____

_____

_____

2. I am open to exploring options. ❑ Yes ❑ No

_____

_____

_____

3. I creatively search for ways to obtain my goals. ❑ Yes   ❑ No

_____

_____

_____

4. I follow through on the commitments I make. ❑ Yes   ❑ No

_____

_____

_____

5. I learn and practice behaviors that enhance my confidence. ❑ Yes   ❑ No

_____

_____

_____

_____

6. I take initiative to keep in contact with my mentor. ❑ Yes   ❑ No

_____

_____

_____

_____

7. I am proactive in the important elements of my relationship. ❑ Yes   ❑ No

_____

_____

_____

8. I take the initiative in creating the mentoring agenda. ❑ Yes   ❑ No

_____

_____

_____

_____

CASE STUDY: The Fagan Factor

Jacqui was very pleased when she was assigned to be mentored by Nick in a formal mentoring program at work. Jacqui had expressed an interest in moving into sales work since she discovered that the company provided a great deal of training and that they reimbursed tuition expenses for job-related courses. She saw these opportunities as a way to compensate for her weak academic background.

Nick was considered a rapidly rising star—a young man on the go in the company's sales force. Jacqui believed she could learn a great deal from Nick, and their early relationship seemed to bear this out. Nick seemed to be all that Jacqui wanted to be herself: self-confident, sophisticated, popular, and at ease with everyone. Jacqui saw Nick as an ideal role model.

Nick was eager to teach Jacqui the ropes of the sales game and to teach her what he called the "keys to the product lines." For the first two months as Nick's mentee, Jacqui alternated between feeling overwhelmed by the pace of her learning, and amazed at how much she had learned in such a short time. It even seemed that some of Nick's charisma had rubbed off on her. People in the plant began to show a respect and even deference toward her—something that Jacqui had never known before.

However, when Nick took Jacqui on some sales calls to other cities they partied with clients a great deal during the evenings. Jacqui concluded that her mentor had expensive taste. Later, Nick wanted her to pad her expense account and "contribute to the festivities." Jacqui felt uncomfortable with this and resisted. Nick got angry and said that Jacqui should carry her part of the load.

Jacqui began to suspect that more than padding was going on when they discussed some of the items for the expense account. Then she remembered several "private conversations" Nick had with some clients after he sent Jacqui on some errands.

CONTINUED

CONTINUED

Analysis

Fagan was a character in the Charles Dickens novel *Oliver Twist*. He took in street children, fed them, gave them a place to stay, and taught them a skill for surviving in 19th century London—picking pockets. Of course, the children didn't get to keep the money they stole. Though some regarded Fagan as a mentor, that is certainly not how mentoring is thought of in the purest definition. By definition, a mentoring relationship has beneficial effects. In reality, many of the children taken in by Fagan would wind up going to prison.

1. Assess Jacqui's options at this point:

   _____

   _____

   _____

   _____

2. Review your definition of mentor and decide if Nick is a mentor.
   ❑ Yes   ❑ No

   If you think he is, how would you describe the kind of mentor he is?

   _____

   _____

   _____

3. If you were Jacqui, what would you do?

   _____

   _____

   _____

   _____

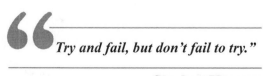

"Try and fail, but don't fail to try."

–Stephen Kaggwa

Part Summary

In this part, you learned how to use **seven** effective mentee skills. You learned how to ask **productive questions**. Next, you learned how to develop **triple level listening skills**, and to use **trust** as your glue. You learned to overcome the **awe** factor, and to **resolve** or manage **differences**. Then, you learned how to capture the **gifts** of learning. Finally, you learned how to **internalize** the learning.

Building a Productive Relationship

"*Man cannot discover new oceans unless he has the courage to lose sight of the shore.*"

–Andre Gide

In this part:

Build a Productive Relationship

A successful and effective mentoring partnership usually doesn't happen automatically. It usually requires planned and purposeful effort if you really want to maximize the impact of mentoring.

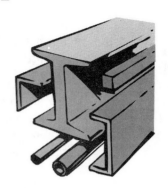

Experience and research tell us that there are characteristics, behaviors, and attitudes that help form and maintain a healthy and productive mentoring relationship. Here are some of those behaviors.

A productive relationship requires that:

▶ Both partners assume shared levels of initiative and risks.

▶ There is a punishment-free environment.

▶ Both participants collaboratively set agreed-upon goals.

▶ Both participants agree to provide continuous constructive feedback.

▶ Partners deal effectively with unmet objectives or expectations.

Elements of an Effective Partnership

▶ Mutual respect

▶ Increased mentee productivity and empowerment

▶ Open mindedness – willingness to be influenced

▶ Trust

▶ Dependable behaviors and commitments

▶ Honesty and frankness

▶ Constructive confrontation for all issues

▶ Commitment to mutual goals

▶ Finding common ground

▶ Mutual satisfaction for the partnership

▶ Preparation for career competition

▶ The sharing of values – what's important for each other

Look at these two lists again and check the items you think are going to be the easiest to do. Circle the ones that you think will require more effort on your part.

The next step is to share the lists with your mentor.

Form the Mentoring Relationship

All relationships have a beginning. For the mentoring relationship to start off with the best momentum and the highest clarity, pay attention to "forming" the relationship. Here are some steps to consider.

1 Communicate to your mentor why you want this relationship. If this is a formal relationship in which management has set the objectives, you might personally want to stress those objectives that are most important to you. Ask for your mentor's reaction.

2 Based on what you shared in step 1, ask your mentor what he or she thinks are his or her strongest suits. Ideally, you both would discuss the alignment between the mentor's strengths and your needs/wants.

3 Write these down. Both of you should have copies. It will be important to refer back to these later in the relationship.

4 At this stage, you might want to adjourn so both can think about the potential relationship. Meet again within a week and decide if both of you wish to proceed with the mentoring process.

YOUR MENTORING NEEDS

As you think about mentoring, try to write as many of the things that you need or want in this relationship.

_____

_____

_____

What are some specific questions that you could ask the potential mentor that will give you the information you need to know if this is a good match?

_____

_____

_____

Create Guiding Principles

Now that you have met with your potential mentor and you believe you would like to proceed, the critical next step is to establish guiding principles. These are the behaviors that the two of you will commit to and will hold each other accountable for. Without guiding principles, both partners will form assumptions that will create problems later. Here are some possible candidates for your guiding principles list.

We the mentor and mentee agree to the following behaviors as core to our mentoring relationship:

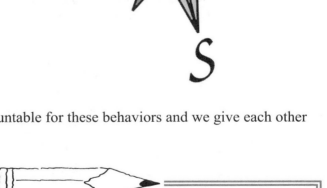

- ▶ Honesty
- ▶ Fairness
- ▶ Candor
- ▶ Constructive feedback
- ▶ Willingness to be influenced
- ▶ Openness to new ideas
- ▶ Trust of intent
- ▶ Confidentiality
- ▶ Patience
- ▶ Responsiveness
- ▶ Initiative
- ▶ Follow-up

We agree to hold each other accountable for these behaviors and we give each other permission in advance to do so.

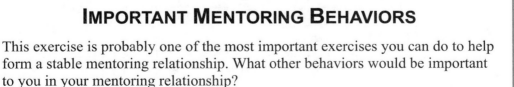

IMPORTANT MENTORING BEHAVIORS

This exercise is probably one of the most important exercises you can do to help form a stable mentoring relationship. What other behaviors would be important to you in your mentoring relationship?

_____

_____

General Relationship Guidelines

It is wise to learn from those that have gone before you in mentoring relationships. Here are some general guidelines that have proven effective for mentoring experiences. Decide for yourself if you would be wise to adopt them for your mentoring relationship.

- ❏ The relationship is voluntary (for informal mentoring).

- ❏ In a work context, be sure to find out if there are established mentoring guidelines that you can use or are required to use.

- ❏ Mentoring is best done when the mentor is not the manager or direct supervisor.

- ❏ A mentor's guidance and counsel never supersedes that of the mentee's supervisor in matters that are the supervisor's responsibility.

- ❏ Mentors and mentees should attend some type of mentoring-related training.

- ❏ The partners mutually develop a mentoring agreement and adhere to it.

- ❏ Both partners are actively involved in the process.

- ❏ Either party can end the relationship any time.

- ❏ Both parties agree to a wrap-up final feedback session to mark the official ending of the relationship.

"That's my previous mentee. His biggest problem was being risk averse."

RELATIONSHIP GUIDELINES

1. Use the preceding list as a starting point for establishing ground rules by checking any to which you and your mentor agree.

2. Can you think of general relationship guidelines other than those in the list that would be important for the success of your mentoring relationship?

_____

_____

_____

_____

_____

3. Use the space below to list any additional organizational ground rules that you are aware of and any others you and your mentor establish and to which you both agree.

_____

_____

_____

_____

_____

_____

_____

" *Have the courage to say no. Have the courage to face the truth. Do the right thing because it is right. These are the magic keys to living your life with integrity.* "

–W. Clement Stone

Establish Procedures for Meetings

Early in the mentoring relationship you and your mentor should establish operating procedures for meetings. In most formal programs it is suggested that you:

▶ Meet once a week to ensure that frequent and frank communication forms the basis for the relationship.

▶ Establish a meeting duration of somewhere between 30 minutes and 60 minutes for most meetings, so as to not unduly burden either partner.

▶ Decide who will set up meetings. Volunteering to do this can be a useful way to give something back to your mentor.

▶ Create a formal agenda for your meetings. This is beneficial for partnerships because over time, neither person will remember everything that has been addressed, agreed to, or is in need of follow-up.

Key questions to ask:

▶ How long are we committing to?

▶ How will we know when it is over?

▶ How often will we meet?

▶ How will we know if we are successful?

▶ How much time will we spend?

▶ Where will we meet?

▶ When will we meet? Over lunch, during work, or outside of work? A mix?

▶ Preferred day, hour, location?

▶ What are the parameters for calling and not calling each other?

▶ What are reasonable expectations for responding to email and phone calls?

▶ What do we do if a meeting has to be canceled or rescheduled?

Of course, exchanging contact information such as email, work, and home phone and cell phone is important.

Remember that the greater the clarity here, the fewer issues later.

The Spectrum of Mentor & Mentee Interactions

As mentee and mentor, decide what kind of mentoring relationship will best meet the goals, needs, and outcomes that you have identified. There is a broad range of mentoring relationship types, so be clear about where you and mentor will begin.

The spectrum below describes types of mentoring relationships.

Situational Responses	Informal Relationship	Formal or Highly Structured Program
Isolated, specific acts by mentor to meet current mentee needs	Interpersonal agreement or understanding for mentor to help mentee, usually in specific areas	Structured program to meet organizational or personal goals

The mentoring relationship could begin at one point in the spectrum and then transition to a different one. For example, starting in an informal mentoring relationship, a mentee might find that s/he needs more structure. In this case, a formal program might be more appropriate. In another case, a formal mentoring relationship might feel too restrictive for both partners to fulfill the demands of such a structured agreement. Maybe an informal or even situational relationship would be better. A healthy relationship and good communication guidelines allow the dialogue needed to make sure the relationship is as fluid and as structured as it needs to be.

▶ A mentoring relationship may shift or evolve over time and move along the spectrum if the partners so choose.

▶ Mentees trained to function effectively across the total spectrum can adapt to a variety of individual needs and opportunities.

▶ A mentee could have several types of mentoring relationships operating at any given time with different individuals. We recommend focusing only on one major mentoring relationship at a time.

In case you haven't noticed, flexibility and adaptability are key to effectively navigating the mentoring relationship.

The Evolution of the Partnership

As shown by the spectrum on the previous page, a mentoring relationship can be:

▶ A single response to a specific situation

▶ An informal relationship between two people

▶ A highly structured, formal program arranged by an organization

Most mentoring relationships evolve over time, depending on the impact of the initial experience. Mentors and mentees often become friends, which means that in the future they can approach each other for mentoring on an as-needed basis. Such relationships can be long-distance or local, long-lasting or exist for specific purposes.

Examples of long-term partnerships

▶ Two Red Cross volunteers communicate weekly by Skype and follow-up with email. Being separated 6,000 miles doesn't stop them from having a productive and valuable mentoring relationship. They are face to face once a year during the annual Red Cross meeting.

▶ Two business people meet by accident at a luncheon and became fast friends. They meet at that same restaurant when one of them needs to talk something over or explore new ideas. They have been doing this for over 25 years.

▶ An engineer has mentored technical personnel in informal relationships throughout his long career. He has been credited with greatly strengthening the company's technical staff. He has since trained others how to mentor and now a growing number of mentors are available to help new hires.

▶ An HIV/AIDS worker in Thailand writes in her daily blog about the sorrow that she experiences and the occasional triumphs that do occur. A long-time colleague and unofficial mentor located in South America reads her blog and provides helpful reflection and contemplation for her to consider. She has found this extremely helpful.

As you can see, the world is a global community in which there is unlimited potential for reaching out and learning from others or being supported. If there is something you need from someone on just about any topic, today's technology makes it available at your fingertips.

Mentoring can be an excellent vehicle for making this happen.

Types of Mentoring Relationships

Each of the relationship options and their characteristics are described here. Each of the three types has its own unique traits:

▶ Formal

▶ Informal

▶ Situations

Formal

General Traits

▶ Can be voluntary or not

▶ Measurably productive

▶ Source of a developing relationship/friendship

▶ Systematic, structured

▶ Institutionalized

▶ Ongoing

▶ Most traditional of the three

Characteristics

▶ Driven by organizational or sometimes personal needs

▶ Focused on achieving organizational or personal goals

▶ Often has a method for matching mentors with mentees

▶ Of fixed duration, based on outcomes

▶ Sponsored or sanctioned by the organization

Often Includes

▶ Monitoring of program

▶ Measurement of results

▶ Focus on goals/outcomes of a special group or possibly an individual

▶ Specially designed organizational interventions

▶ Ideally, a sense of mutuality

Informal

General Traits

▶ Voluntary

▶ Just-in-time response to mentee needs

▶ Can be professional or personal in nature

▶ Loosely structured

▶ Flexible

Characteristics

▶ Caring, sharing, or helping

▶ A mutual acceptance of roles

▶ A path to developing respect and/or friendship

▶ Heavily reliant on mentor's knowledge, skills, abilities, and competence

Often Includes

▶ Mentee-revealed needs

▶ Periodic assessment of results

▶ Mentor having more than one role relationship with mentee (supervisor, friend, teacher)

▶ Team mentoring with emphasis on one-on-one interaction

▶ Ideally, a sense of mutuality

Situational

General Traits

▶ Short, specific, isolated episodes

▶ Spontaneous, off-the-cuff interventions

▶ Seemingly random

▶ Often casual

▶ Creative, innovative

Characteristics

▶ Responsive to current needs/situations

▶ Mentor-initiated intervention

▶ A one-time event or a repeated set of unconnected one-time events

▶ The mentee's responsibility to use lessons offered

▶ Not based on clearly defined expectations or outcomes

Often Includes

▶ Distinct, beneficial effects on the mentee's life or lifestyle

▶ Network of mentors to call upon

▶ Mentee's increased sensitivity to opportunities

▶ Mentee assessing results later

▶ A memorable and lasting learning experience

▶ Ideally, a sense of mutuality

As you consider the kind of mentoring experience that you would benefit most from, review these traits and characteristics. One technique might be for you to circle the items most important to you and see what kind of mentoring relationship emerges. Share this list with your potential mentor and see if you can construct a relationship that is unique and somewhat of a hybrid.

Remember that the mentee needs to take initiative.

MENTEE RESPONSIBILITIES

In informal and situational mentoring, the relationship is the most free of structure. In a formal mentoring program there may be pressure to promise specific outcomes and produce measurable results. Review the following list and check behaviors that you think will help you achieve the best results. Share this list with your mentor. It will help make sure you both are better aligned at the beginning of the relationship.

I will:

❑ Decide what I need from the mentoring relationship.

❑ Commit to regular/frequent meetings with my mentor.

❑ Share my needs, goals, fears, concerns and desires with my mentor.

❑ Follow through on all commitments that I make.

❑ Make sure we mutually set realistic expectations for our relationship.

❑ Share failures as well as successes.

❑ Be sincere, open, and receptive to mentor input.

❑ Accept it if my mentor is unable to meet some of my aspirations.

❑ Initiate frequent and steady contact as appropriate and as agreed.

❑ Explore options openly with my mentor.

❑ Share important feelings that I experience along the way.

❑ Invest my energies in making the relationship a success.

❑ Search for and be open to new ways to achieve my objectives.

❑ Be receptive to my mentor's point of view.

❑ Mentally review, summarize, and internalize the knowledge, skills, and abilities I receive from my mentor—and make them mine!

> *Reach high, for stars lie hidden in your soul.*
> *Dream deep, for every dream precedes the goal."*
>
> **–Pamela Vaull Starr**

Align Expectations

The most critical element of the mentoring relationship is aligning expectations. Some mentees assume that because their mentor is more experienced, better educated, or has greater access to organizational resources, the mentor should be able to teach them anything or solve any problem. This assumption can lead the relationship to a parent/child situation,

which is not effective mentoring. A mentor has strengths and challenges just like every other human being. Most committed mentors will respond to inquiries as best they can based on what they have learned or experienced. Remember, however, that they are not infallible.

Mentoring is neither a marriage nor an adoption, yet mentoring can founder when unrealistic—or worse, unstated—expectations are held by one of the partners.

These expectations may originate from our cultural norms and come out unconsciously. In a conventional marriage, for instance, a husband often expects certain conduct from his wife, and vice versa, without ever discussing these assumptions. A mentee will most likely expect certain things from a mentor. Make these expectations explicit to avoid disrupting the relationship.

For example, a mentee might inappropriately expect a mentor to:

▶ Help the mentee achieve a promotion.

▶ Give the mentee advice.

▶ Be an infinite font of wisdom.

▶ Advance the mentee's cause with the mentor's friends and associates.

Any of these might be contrary to the program's goals, the culture of the organization, or the needs of the individual. The mentor and mentee need to discuss their respective motives and expectations.

The mentor and mentee should not proceed farther with the mentoring relationship until their expectations are aligned. Skipping this step will damage the relationship later.

Take the initiative. Be bold and get clear and aligned on expectations.

ALIGNING MENTORING EXPECTATIONS

Use this exercise to get clear and get aligned with expectations in the mentoring relationship.

1. List your expectations of and assumptions about your mentor:

_____

_____

_____

2. Ask your mentor to list his/her expectations of and assumptions about you, the mentee:

_____

_____

_____

3. How would you characterize the alignment of these two?

_____

_____

_____

4. Discuss #1, 2, and 3 with your mentor and decide how to make sure these expectations and assumptions are as aligned as possible.

_____

_____

_____

5. Whatever you decide in #4 should become part of your mentoring agreement and your guiding principles. Success with this exercise will be an excellent sign that you two have what it takes to create a very meaningful and productive mentoring experience.

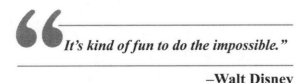

It's kind of fun to do the impossible."

–Walt Disney

Giving Back: Balancing the Relationship

A study involving 312 mentors asked what they hoped to get from the mentoring relationship. Many of the survey responses relied on their observations of what their mentee did and said about a given experience or bit of special learning.

Some of the findings showed that mentors hoped to:

▶ Improve their leadership abilities.

▶ Experience the pleasure of helping someone succeed.

▶ Have a high-quality teaching experience.

▶ Enjoy the expression of a mentee's appreciation.

▶ Know that they are doing something important.

In general, responses to the survey focused on a relatively small, rather simple list of satisfiers. Yet one satisfier stood out above all the rest: Mentors wanted to know that they

"…had made an important, long-lasting, positive change in another person's life, something that would help their mentees move forward into their future."

These are the items that mentors receive in return for their generosity. These "satisfiers" are what a mentee gives back to a mentor. This giving back can foster a deep sense of mutuality in the relationship.

To a large degree the mentor gives during the beginning and throughout the mentoring relationship. The biggest giving from the mentee comes after the mentoring is over. Experienced, effective mentors know about this delayed give-back and are usually confident in themselves to know it will come.

GIVING BACK TO YOUR MENTOR

What is your reaction to the concept that you, the mentee, will be giving back to the mentor? Be sure to share this with your mentor.

_____

_____

_____

_____

The Emergent Property: Synergy

It might sound corny to say that mentoring makes magic happen. However, that is how many mentoring partners describe the experience.

The discipline of Systems Thinking includes the concept of "emergent property." An emergent property is something that appears as a result of other things that occur. One example would be a rainbow. A rainbow appears only because of the way you are standing, the placement of the sun, and the falling of the rain. If any one of those items is not there, there is no rainbow.

Transportation is another emergent property. The movement of a car is an emergent property of hundreds of other systems and parts working together.

Mentors and mentees often observe powerful, positive transformations in themselves. One mentor described the results of the relationship as "absolutely incredible; a major transformation that has changed me forever." This sentiment is another example of an emergent property. This "major transformation" emerged as a result of the many elements of a successful mentoring experience.

Others are impressed by the productivity, friendship, and other remarkable changes that occur in their lives. Both mentors and mentees report these kinds of gains—these kinds of emergent properties. Two people who really listen to each other, who work at helping each other, and who are concerned for each other can hardly fail to create synergy. What grows between them is a relationship that is more than the sum of its parts.

In addition to the gains of the mentor and mentee, the employer benefits by the ideas and the improved performance of the mentee. Employees in these programs tend to be more cooperative and more focused on beneficial results.

Synergy describes a situation in which the whole is greater than the sum of the parts. The synergy that flows from mentoring benefits just about everyone involved.

Can you think of any other emergent properties in your life?

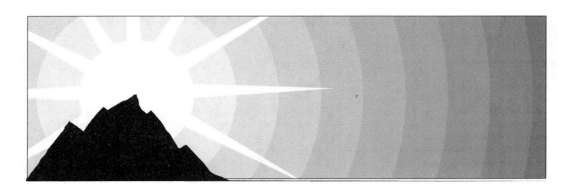

CASE STUDY: When Needs Are Not Met

Johanne received a medical degree from the National University of Haiti. With the help of her church she was able to enter the United States through an exception granted to immigrants who possess technical and professional skills needed in the United States.

Johanne took the standard U.S. examination for people who attended a foreign medical school, but failed. She was told that she was close to passing, but that English—which she had just learned in college—was her great weakness. This was demonstrated on the exam by her inability to answer some of the questions.

She quickly accepted temporary work in a local hospital as a technician, although language problems held her back. She believed that the opportunity to work in a medical high-tech environment would prove valuable when she finally passed her medical exam. Shortly after joining the hospital, she was invited to join a mentoring program, and accepted. She was assigned to Dr. Dobson's "protégé" program.

Johanne had three primary concerns that she thought a mentor could either help her with, or at least point her in the right direction:

1. She wanted to be able to speak and write English more effectively.

2. She wanted to discover resources that could help her pass the medical examinations.

3. She needed guidance on how and where to pursue further schooling to become a cardiologist.

Unfortunately, Dr. Dobson most often took up much of the weekly mentor/mentee meetings avoiding her questions and telling long, involved stories about his own experiences, which seemed to bear no connection to what Johanne wanted to achieve. She suspected that it was difficult for him to understand her and that he considered the effort a waste of his time. One day she overheard him say, "She's one of those foreigners we've become so dependent on."

CONTINUED

CONTINUED

1. Based upon what you have read in this case study, what are your impressions of the current mentoring relationship?

_____

_____

_____

_____

2. Should this partnership continue? Please explain your answer.

_____

_____

_____

_____

3. What could Dr. Dobson do to be more effective as a mentor?

_____

_____

_____

4. How much responsibility does Johanne have in this current situation?

_____

_____

_____

_____

Part Summary

In this part, you learned how to **build** and **form** a productive mentoring relationship. Then, you learned how to create **guiding principles**. You learned how to establish procedures for **meetings**. Next, you learned the **spectrum** of mentoring interactions, the **evolution** of the mentoring partnership, and the **types** of mentoring partnerships. You learned how to **align** expectations and how to **give back**. Finally, you learned that **synergy** is the **emergent property** of a mentoring relationship.

Fine Tuning & Transitioning the Mentoring Relationship

" *Learning how to learn is life's most important skill.* "

–Tony Buzan

In this part:

- ▶ Creating Balance in Your Life
- ▶ Identifying and Using Learning Styles
- ▶ Workplace Diversity: Gaining a New Perspective
- ▶ Embracing Change
- ▶ Overcoming Inertia in the Organization
- ▶ Transitioning/Ending the Relationship

Creating Balance in Your Life

Changes that occur during mentoring can sometimes cause stress. Stress can seep into the mentoring relationship without our conscious knowledge. One of the things that a mentor picks up on in a mentoring relationship is the mentee's level of stress. Sometimes the mentor can serve as a kind of mirror to reflect back to the mentee what s/he sees. Sometimes it takes another person to see the stress that we cannot.

Meeting our common needs can counter stress. Some needs are listed below.

People need:

- ▶ Satisfying work
- ▶ Good health and wellness
- ▶ Financial security
- ▶ Some level of hope for the future
- ▶ Relaxation and ways to rejuvenate
- ▶ Nourishment for their higher spirit
- ▶ Awareness of how the world is changing
- ▶ A feeling of being connected to family and friends
- ▶ A feeling of orderliness in their professional, personal, or family life

LIST OF NEEDS

Identify any items you would like to add to your own list of needs:

_____

_____

To what degree are you lacking in any of these areas?

_____

_____

What can you do to address any of these items to help create more balance?

_____

_____

Identifying and Using Learning Styles

Mentoring is a process of learning. The mentee, with the careful guidance of a mentor, learns new ways of thinking and doing through the mentoring experience. There are three primary ways people learn.

The three learning styles are:

▶ **Visual**: *learning by seeing*

▶ **Auditory**: *learning by hearing*

▶ **Tactile**: *learning by doing*

Each of us has a preferred (primary) way to absorb information and skills. We often also have a secondary learning style that we find useful.

In mentoring this becomes important because mentors who are primarily visual learners, and secondarily auditory, are likely to communicate with pictures or diagrams. Mentees who are primarily tactile and secondarily auditory might find diagrams hard to understand. Mentors also might not appreciate a need for hands-on learning. The partners should discuss individual learning styles early in the relationship.

LEARNING STYLES

What are your preferred learning styles?

Primary _____

Secondary _____

Why do think these are your primary and secondary learning styles?

_____

_____

Just for practice, try to guess the learning behaviors of another person. Who could help and what clues might there be to help you?

_____

_____

_____

Workplace Diversity: Gaining a New Perspective

Today's Global, Green, Information-Driven, High-Tech Era is a rich potpourri of human beings collaborating every day to create value in the marketplace and keep the world's economic engine running. This potpourri of talented, diverse individuals provides tremendous opportunities for mentoring because of their diversity.

One of the ways that companies have found to stay competitive is to continually acquire and broaden knowledge and skills. Today's workplace diversity provides opportunities to expand personally and professionally. In many cases, you can learn more from someone who is different from you than from someone who is like you.

The best mentoring results often come when a mentor is very different from the mentee. Find ways to embrace diversity. Soak in as much of that diverse thought and perspective as possible to enrich your own ways of doing things.

GAINING A NEW PERSPECTIVE

Do you see value in being mentored by someone who is different from you? Why?

_____

_____

_____

_____

As you think about being mentored by someone from a different culture, race, background, gender, and so on, what kinds of things come to mind—positive and negative? Be sure to talk these through with you mentor.

_____

_____

_____

Embracing Change

You will be changed in some ways by the mentoring process. We encourage mentees to look beyond the usual fear of change and instead welcome it as a path to someplace new—personally and professionally. Here are some ways to help understand change.

▶ People are not resistant to change. They only resist being confused about change. They want to know the why of it and how it will affect them.

▶ People want some level of control over change that affects them.

▶ If the change is understandable and supportable, people will want to contribute to the process—to become part of it.

We need time and energy to adjust to the stress that sometimes comes with change. From our point of view, well managed and acknowledged stress is a small price to pay for the tremendous growth potential that comes with each change opportunity. Watch for the changes that come your way. Embrace them and they will, with your mentor's guidance and support, treat you well—probably for a lifetime.

POSITIVE AND NEGATIVE CHANGE

Think back to how you have experienced change in your life. List some changes that you thought were positive and then list the negative ones.

Positive changes and the impact they had on you:

_____

_____

_____

Negative changes and the impact they had on you:

_____

_____

_____

Even what we think of as negative change usually offers a learning opportunity and can positively shape us. The choice is always ours.

Overcoming Inertia in the Organization

The law of inertia says a body in motion tends to remain in motion and that a body at rest tends to remain at rest. Inertia simply means a resistance or disinclination to change. Within an organization, this inertia can impact your mentoring process.

Common reasons for inertia within an organization are:

► A desire to get the job done the way it's always been done

► Habit: no need for decision making and risk taking. Why bother?

► Fear of unknown consequences

► Fear of failure if old failures were punished

► Concern for lack of time and other resources

► Fear that change may cause failure in other areas

► Implied criticism—may be interpreted to mean someone is doing something wrong

Dealing with these sometimes strong resistant forces can be challenging. As a progressive-thinking mentee, don't get discouraged. Move forward. Here are some suggestions when facing resistance.

► Provide clear and concise reasons why the change is beneficial.

► Project confident vocal support of productive change.

► Initiate open-ended discussions about changes that affect similar organizations.

► Look for opportunities to join others in adapting to the changing world.

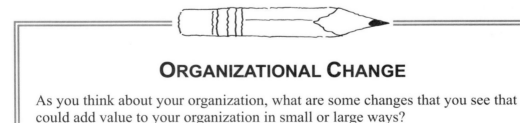

ORGANIZATIONAL CHANGE

As you think about your organization, what are some changes that you see that could add value to your organization in small or large ways?

_____

_____

_____

Remember, change is challenging but that is not a reason to not try.

Transitioning / Ending the Relationship

As discussed earlier in this book, you and your mentor should have discussed how you will end your mentoring relationship.

Sometimes the best sign of when to end the relationship is when one or both of you believe: *"I've gotten what I need and it is time for me to meet new challenges. Thanks for your help!"*

Some mentoring relationships have a specific end time, which makes the decision easier. A non-specific date should be discussed with candor and honesty when either person thinks it is time to end or transition the relationship.

Ending or transitioning the mentoring relationship is the last critical step in the evolution of the mentoring process. It brings a transition to the relationship.

Some things to consider as you meet—and we strongly recommend that you have a final meeting—to close or transition the mentoring relationship:

▶ Reflect on the process overall. What was it like for the two people?

▶ What were the highlights?

▶ What were the challenges and how did we handle them?

▶ What did we learn that is actionable, meaning what will do differently going forward?

▶ What kind of relationship would we like to have now that this part of the relationship is over?

▶ How shall we celebrate for our accomplishment?

We know from experience and research that this "final" meeting with the specific purpose of transitioning the relationship provides a wealth of benefits. Please be sure to reap these benefits as a topping-off of all of the other powerful elements of mentoring.

HONORING A MENTORING RELATIONSHIP

What are some ways the two of you can honor and celebrate the ending or transitioning of your mentoring relationship?

_____

_____

_____

How lucky I am to have something that makes saying goodbye so hard."

–Carol Sobieski and Thomas Meehan, from _Annie_

"For the final phase of my mentoring program, I'm sending you up the creek without a paddle."

CASE STUDY: The Problem with "Champions"

A month after graduating from college, Janel accepted a job with a federal agency in his chosen field. He arrived on his first morning ready for work, but also somewhat nervous, since this was his first "real" job.

Janel and eighteen other new employees received a brief orientation, including a film on the agency, its structure, and mission. Each participant was also given a folder listing "all of the things you need to know"—including instructions on how to complete electronic time sheets, a Google map of local bus routes, key agency phone numbers and email addresses, and other valuable information.

The big surprise of the day came when they were told that they had been singled out for a new six-month mentoring program where they would be rotated through several jobs and be mentored by the manager in each department. When they were given the list of participants in the program, Janel noticed they were referred to as organizational "champions—the high-potential people expected to lead the agency some day."

Although Janel felt flattered by the attention he was receiving, he was somewhat uncomfortable when he thought over the agency's plans for him and other interns. His concerns were:

▶ He had a technical background, wanted to do "real work" in his specialty and didn't want to "spend six months wandering around," as he put it.

▶ He wondered about the reaction of other employees to his group now that they were being identified as "champions" and the fact that these individuals were to be the leaders of the future.

▶ He wasn't at all sure he wanted to be a "champion" or even a leader/manager.

▶ He also wondered who made this decision. How is it he doesn't know who views him as "high potential"?

▶ He felt as though things were way out of his control or even influence over a massive plan in which he had no input.

CONTINUED

Individuals identified as high-potential performers (and given opportunities and training beyond that of their co-workers) often prove disappointing in later performance. At least this is what some research suggests. For example, in succession planning for bright young people, academic performance was the basis for inducting them into the program, though performance in a corporate or government environment requires different skill sets. This means that the skills might not be as transferable as originally thought.

Janel didn't want to seem ungrateful, but he had several concerns that he needed to discuss with his mentors. Think about what you would do if you were in Janel's place.

Should Janel try to get out of the program? ❑ Yes ❑ No

Why or why not?

_____

_____

If yes, what approach should Janel take with his mentor(s) to bring up the topic of getting out of the program and starting technical work?

_____

_____

_____

Janel's colleagues that were not designated as champions could infer that they are inferior in some way. What if anything should Janel do about this?

_____

_____

_____

Janel has his sights set on a different career path—what should he do about this?

_____

_____

_____

Part Summary

In this part, you learned how to create **balance** in your life. Next, you learned how to identify and use different **learning styles**. You learned about workplace **diversity** and learned how to **embrace change**. Then, you learned how to **overcome inertia** in the organization. Finally, you learned how to **transition** or **end** the relationship.

A P P E N D I X

Final Thoughts

For thousands of years mentoring played a role in the development of human civilization and evolution. There must be something to it if it has survived all these years.

Organizations that invest in mentoring reap rewards well beyond the time frame of any informal or formal mentoring effort. Once the seeds have been planted, things begin to grow everywhere in terms of productivity, job satisfaction, creativity, problem solving, effectiveness, efficiencies, and teamwork.

A few things to remember about mentoring:

▶ Mentoring tends to be most productive when it operates as an adult-to-adult partnership.

▶ The partnership is voluntary on both sides—even in formal, organization-sponsored programs.

▶ To be effective, both partners must be committed to it and willing to do their part.

▶ Mentees have a responsibility to manage their own development and career. They need to study and practice the skills that will foster a good mentoring relationship.

▶ Being mentored is not a training program and not an entitlement. Mentoring is the act of going above and beyond the ordinary to produce powerful, positive change in another person.

▶ The center piece of mentoring is constructive feedback in both directions.

Here's to your success at first being a mentee and later on returning the favor by offering others your gifts by being a mentor. Never forget what it was like to be a mentee. There will be a time when you will recall it fondly as you take someone on and provide them with guidance and caring and help shape their life for the better.

Best of luck to you!

> *To know when to go away and when to come closer is the key to any lasting relationship.*

–**Doménico Cieri Estrada**

Additional Reading

Crisp 50-Minute Series books:

Bonet, Diana. *The Business of Listening.*

Hathaway, Patti. *Feedback Skills for Leaders.*

Kravitz, Michael and Susan Schubert. *Emotional Intelligence Works.*

Lloyd, Sam. *Self-Empowerment.*

Minor, Marianne. *Coaching and Counseling.*

Scott, Cynthia D. and Dennis T. Jaffe. *Change Management.*

Other related reading:

Bell, Chip R. *Managers as Mentors.* San Francisco, CA: Berret-Koehler Publishers, Inc., 1996.

Cook, Marshall J. *Effective Coaching.* New York, NY: McGraw-Hill, 1999.

Cottrel, David, *Monday Morning Mentoring* (Kindle Edition), Harper Collins e-books, 2006.

Douglas, Christina A. *Formal Mentoring Programs in Organizations: An Annotated Bibliography,* Adobe e-books.

Ensher, Ellen A. & Murphy, Susan E. *Power Mentoring: How Successful Mentors and Proteges Get the Most out of Their Relationships,* San Francisco, CA: Jossey-Bass, 2005.

Evans, Thomas W *Mentors: Making a Difference in Our Public Schools.* Princeton, NJ: Peterson's Guides, 1992.

Goleman, Daniel. *Emotional Intelligence.* New York, NY: Bantam Books, 1995.

Harvard Business Essentials, *Coaching and Mentoring: How to Develop Top Talent and Achieve Stronger Performance,* Harvard Business School Press, 2004.

Johnson, Brad W., Ridley, Charles, R. *The Elements of Mentoring,* Revised Edition. Macmillan, 2008.

Maxwell, John C. *Mentoring 101.* Nashville, TN: Thomas Nelson Publishers, 2008.

Web Resources

Below are just a few of the many resources available to you via the World Wide Web. This listing is by no means exhaustive. This list is to give you an idea of the various resources that are available to you should you wish to pursue more information online. The items listed below are not for profit organizations. As you can imagine, there are many online resources that are for profit and provide a very wide variety of mentoring information. As is true with any online resource, be wise and be careful before making purchases. We also suggest that no one resource can have the entire scope of mentoring information. It pays to shop around, do good research, compare and contrast, and look into the source itself to try and verify how reliable it is.

▶ www.hsph.harvard.edu/research/chc/harvard-mentoring-project/

Promotes the growth of the mentoring movement with the goal of linking large numbers of young people with adult mentors.

▶ www.mentoring-association.org

The International Mentoring Association: The I MA promotes individual and organization development through mentoring best practices. We serve persons in mentoring in public and private institutions, business and industry. Membership is open to all who support the objectives of the Association.

▶ www.managementhelp.org/guiding/mentrng/mentrng.htm

The Free Management Library provides easy-to-access, clutter-free, comprehensive resources regarding the leadership and management of yourself, other individuals, groups, and organizations. The content is relevant to the vast majority of people, whether they are in large or small for-profit or nonprofit organizations. Over the past 10 years, the Library has grown to be one of the world's largest well-organized collections of these types of resources.

50-Minute™ Series

If you enjoyed this book, we have great news for you.
There are more than 200 books available in the
Crisp Fifty-Minute™ Series.

Subject Areas Include:

Management and Leadership
Human Resources
Communication Skills
Personal Development
Sales and Marketing
Accounting and Finance
Coaching and Mentoring
Customer Service/Quality
Small Business and Entrepreneurship
Writing and Editing

For more information visit us online at

www.CrispSeries.com

VERS